The Last Generation of the Utila
Full Moon
Memories of Paradise
Randy Cardona

This book is dedicated our son Duane Evans Cardona who lived for just four days, yet you taught me so much about myself, good and bad. We will always love and miss you.

To all who buy a copy of this book I thank you. Please allow me to be imperfect in my first attempt at being a (self) published author. In the end it is the story that I hope make this book worth the read.

Much care was taken to spell the names of the many people mentioned in this book but I was unable to verify each one individually. Apologies to any names spelled incorrectly.

Introduction

I was born in paradise.

Yes, I along with the children growing up during the 1960's on the island of Utila in Central America, were all born in paradise. It is the only way to describe the growing up experience that we had during this period. We were born on a seven mile long by three mile wide-island hidden in the Caribbean Sea.

No world maps or globes would even recognize Utila. It was just too small and insignificant. But to us, the children, it was almost perfect. It was paradise and it was bursting with a great array of sounds, smells and colors. All were natural. We had the best of what nature had to offer. The only thing we did not have was technology, and that was the key, as you could not have at the same time.

Utila, tucked away anonymously in the Caribbean Sea, is located off the coast and belonging to the Republic of Honduras in Central America. It seemed like we were living in a cocoon all by ourselves, separated from the mainland by 18 miles of ocean and by light years from the industrialized world. As children we knew very little about what was happening beyond our small island and the outside knew even less about us.

All we had was "God and Nature," I heard an old man say, I think it was Mr. Theodore Castillo, one night down by The Corner at the center of town. Yes, all we had was "God and nature". They both played a key role in our lives on a daily basis.

Utila, along with the islands of Bonaca/Guanaja, Roatan, and a few other islands make up the Bay Islands of Honduras and were British possessions until September 15th, 1821. But even after more than 100 years of being under the Spanish Honduran flag, the English tradition lived on strong during this time in the Bay Islands.

The official language of the country was Spanish but the islanders spoke only English when not in school. The island people were a mixture from England, Jamaica and The Cayman Islands. The islanders were 99% black or white while the mainland was made up of 99% Spanish, Indian or mixed. We went bare feet all the time and we lived off the land and the sea and as one with nature.

We, the generation born in the 50's and 60's, were destined to be the last generation of the Utila full moon. We would be that generation that slowly began to see the reliance on nature, including the full moon, greatly diminish and give way to the generation of modern technology and everything that came along with it.

We would be that generation that bridged the gap between the past (the old) and the new. But during this period in time we the children of Utila were living in paradise.

No generation before us and no generation after ours could fully understand the life we had, which at times was primitive but it was always simple.

The list of things we did not have was long. We had no telephones or televisions, no cars or trucks, no motorcycles, no indoor plumbing, no newspapers, no banks, no medical center, no doctors, no certified dentist, and the list went on. Anything connected to technology was in short supply. The list of things we did have was short. Like Mr. Theodore said that night, "God and Nature".

We had the crystal clear and always warm Caribbean Sea and the fertile land. We lived directly from them both with an over abundance of seafood, fruits and vegetables. We also had the sun, which gave the island a year round average temperature above 85 degrees. We the children had the most important element to being in paradise, the freedom to enjoy it.

It was a long time ago but I can still remember as if it was yesterday.

I Remember

: Randy Cardona

There was a place,

A long, long time ago,

And far, far away...

We were living in paradise,

on Utila Bay.

Where down on The Corner,

We would gather at night,

To see some fandango in Edwards

Hall...

or maybe a fight,

I can still remember...

I can still remember the sight

Peanuts, "peanole" and a Menga

Holly-holly

I remember Mr. Frank Morgan...

And I remember Ms. Molly.

Stick horse riding cowboys,

Being alive was so much fun;

We had the land, the air, the sea,

And our best friend was the sun.

We were young.

I remember Mr. Foster Cooper...

And I remember Captain Arch,

I remember buying 3 cents sugar...

And five cents starch.

Lisha, Killy and Ms. Lilly Gay,

Break any of The Ten Commandments,

And you knew you had to pay.

I remember...

I remember Utila Bay

We were bare-foot boys,

And those two-shoe girls...

running around town in their hot-

Comb curls.

I remember

And on a Fifteenth of September

Morn'

One   thousand   people   marching

strong

9

"Viva" this and "Viva" that

I can still remember us singing...

the independence song.

Saturdays everyone went swimming,

And next day you had to go to

Sunday school,

Everyone got by one way or the

Other,

living by the Golden Rule

I remember.

Yes there was a place long, long

time ago...

and far, far away,

I remember living in paradise...

I remember Utila Bay.

Chapter One

My family lived on The Hill. Our house was located about a mile from the harbor. It was early 1960's and school was on vacation and I was about 6 years old. It was a great time and place to be a child.

My father Dolores, (it is a long story how he got that name), and mother Rose Marie (Angus) Cardona lived in our house with my sister Lola and myself. Later my parents had another daughter named Linda. They called me "buddo" or Ran, my sister Lola they called her "sista", and my younger sister Linda, "Cuca". My father also had another son, Carlos (Charles Longsworth) by a previous marriage, who lived in Puerto Cortes, on the mainland with his mother.

My father was a proud and good man. He believed in working for everything he had and never relying on anyone. His brothers and sisters were Joseph (McKenzie) Pancho, Peter, Carmen, Maria, Victoria, Elmina, Elozia and Victor. Their parents were Peter and Julia (Forbes) Cardona.

My father worked as a merchant seaman and during this time. He and my mother spoiled my sisters and me. My mother's parents were Joseph and Mannettie Angus. They also had Cleghorn, Sarita (Sara), Irene, Crystalline, Mary Ann and Joseph, who drowned on a small sailboat, which was on its way to the mainland with two other men. They were carrying a load of "buttonwood" posts to sell.

I lay awake this night in my bed unable to sleep. I had on a pair of white pair of underwear and no shirt. It was a hot night, even by Utila norms. The wooden window was swung open to let in some fresh air but it also allowed the mosquitoes to come in. There were no fans or air conditioners and the island's electricity went off at 9 p.m. It was close to midnight.

The night was dark and quiet but so much happening outside my window. There was no "outside" interference so all sounds were natural. The mosquitoes buzzed around my ears making their screeching cries. They would take a bite and I would slap and try to kill them.

I was excited about tomorrow so I didn't pay too much attention to them. My parents would later buy us a see-through mosquito net that hung from the high bedposts or the ceiling and it surrounded the bed right down to the floor, keeping out the mosquitoes.

The darkness was so thick that if you threw a stick out into it, I believe the stick would have gotten stuck. There was no moon tonight, and on Utila after 9 p.m. you really noticed and paid attention to this fact. Dim light from the kerosene lantern on the table in the parlor seeped through the open partition at the top of the walls in my room.

I heard bats quietly zipping through the air. I saw them many times before going from tree to tree and from fruit to fruit. Tonight they were eating their full of ripe mangoes. It was an amazing sight to see them with their silhouetted outstretched wings flying from one mango tree to another, against the backdrop of a moon lit sky.

I heard them making their rounds of taking bites. Tonight the bats singled out the mango trees in our yard and they were feasting, making a kissing kind of a sound.

I heard our horse Black Beauty flapping his long tail against his body as he tried to fend off the mosquitoes. He was a beautiful big black horse. He was tied to a mango tree in the back of the house. He was a headstrong horse and my father would not let me ride him by myself until I was older. But he took me many times riding to farm his piece of land in the bush. I would sit behind my father, holding on with my two arms around his waist.

I heard our young pig grunting and snorting as she breathed deeply in her sleep. She was tied to a post under the house floor. The mosquitoes were bothering all humans and animals.

I heard the sound of a single dry mango leaf drop from the tree and hit the zinc rooftop and then slide down to the ground. The sounds of the night were clear. You could hear for miles especially in the dead of night.

We had five to seven mango trees in our yard, which was connected to my grandmother Mannettie and grand-father Joseph Angus' yard. They lived next door to us with "Uncle", most people knew him as "Cleggie" (Cleghorn). He also worked as a merchant seaman and supported my mother's family while he was at sea. Life was really tough during for the generation before us.

Also living there was my cousin Gilly (Harley Gillian Gregory) and his mother aunt Sarita (Sara Angus) who moved early on to the mainland and became a nurse. She later sent for Gilly whose father was Mr. Rudolph Gregory.

Aunt Sarita (Sara) later married my uncle Apa (Aparicio Herrera) and had two girls, my cousins Melba and Sara. My sisters and I would live with them later in a town called Isleta while my mother in New York and my father worked at sea. We had fun living with them.

The bats were eating all that they could before the morning sun rose. They knew how to find the ripest and sweetest fruits and would just bite off small pieces of a mango and move on to a different one. Tonight they had the pick of the crop and the trees were loaded.

Sometimes when the fruit was just ripe enough, the bat, by biting it would cause the mango to drop to the ground. The next day when you saw those mangoes with a small bite taken out, you knew those were sweet and you would pick them up to eat. We called these mangoes "bat-eaters".

I heard my dog Shaggy restlessly walking around outside. Pets, mainly dogs were never allowed in the house. And cats were only welcomed in the house when there were rats to be caught. There were not a lot of leftovers so the pets had to rely on themselves to hunt for some of their food.

In the distance I heard the loud meowing of what we called a "ram" cat. They were big, "bad", male cats whose sound was a sad, mean, long and scary meow. The "ram" cat meowed all night. I could not go to sleep.

But it was not the sounds outside my window that kept me awake. I could not sleep because I kept thinking about the time I would have when daytime arrived. I planned to go hunting for "wishiwillies" (iguanas) with a couple of older boys who were about 10 to 12 years old. They said I could go with them as long as I did not get in their way. Hunting for iguanas was a rite of passage for all the boys on Utila.

At such young ages we, boys and girls, had freedom to roam the island and could go to so many places all over on our own. I would soon be going hunting in the "bush". I had asked my parents if I could go and they said yes.

The night wore on me. Every now and then I would doze off then wake up and dose off again. Next door to us, the rooster belonging to Ms. Lydia began to crow as he did each day before sunrise. Ms. Lydia and her husband, Mr. Leonidas Bernard lived in their house in back of ours with their children Henry Lewis, Nat, Rody, Grayson, Annette, Julie, Angela and Verona.

The chickens were restless in their coop. They were usually very quiet at night and just wanted to sleep after spending the whole day scavenging for food and water.

Soon all the roosters on the Hill, then those in The Valley began to crow and the morning sun is never far behind the rooster's crow. Shaggy began to bark. I planned to take him with me on the hunt. He was a beautiful medium sized black dog and I loved him.

While lying in my bed I heard my mother go to the bathroom. She was about to begin her daily routine. It was time to empty slop bucket. She and other women would take their slop buckets down to the swamp each morning and empty them. Ours was a five-gallon plastic pail with a metal wire handle and a cover.

The slop bucket was used to store the bathroom waste from the previous 24 hours and then would be dumped in the swamp early each morning. Like most people on Utila during this time, we had no toilets in our house. Most homes either had chamber pots, outhouses and/or slop buckets.

I could still remember when we got our first flushing toilet. I was about 7 or 8 years old. So many children never had something as simple as a flush toilet during our time.

I heard my mother open the back door and walk down the steps with the slop bucket in her hand.

18

I looked out my window to see her head down the Hill to the swamp behind Mr. Georgie (George) and Ms. Judith Gabourel's house. They lived there with their children, Freddie, Margaret (Muggie), Claudia, Carol Cecile (Chi Chi), and Glenn.

Our families were very close at this time as both my father and Mr. Georgie worked as merchant seamen. When their ships were docked in the port of Tela or Puerto Cortes, my mother and Ms. Judith would take the children by boat from Utila to meet them.

Sometimes my family would take the boat, The Mary L, to La Ceiba and then take the train the rest of the way. Then sometimes we would take a boat like The Patsel" straight to the port of Tela or Cortes to meet our father. The boat ride would take anywhere from 8 to 12 hours and would leave at night to arrive in the morning the next day. Many times we were caught in storms on these small boats.

A few minutes later I heard my mother return. She washed the slop bucket by scooping some water with a clean glass or pot from the water barrel.

She then threw some Clorox in the bucket and rinsed it out. She washed her hands. Clorox was used for every type of cleaning or sanitizing. The women of the island "swore" by it.

I heard my mother and father speaking in the kitchen as she began making breakfast. After lighting the stove, the first thing she did was boil water for coffee. On Utila, every woman and man followed a daily routine. The women woke up early, prepared breakfast, got ready for dinner (we did not know about lunch) and then they would prepare for supper.

In between they would clean the house, shop for the next meal's groceries and do the other household chores. The men also followed their same routine every day. Wake up early and eat breakfast, which usually began with a cup of hot coffee, then they would set off to farm their piece of land or to fish, or both: farm in the morning and fish in the afternoon. The same thing happened everyday at the same time.

Saturdays and Sundays were the only days that interrupted the routine of the islanders. If you were an Adventist you took Saturday as your holy day and you rested. If you attended the other churches like the Methodist, Baptist or the Church of God, you took Sundays off to rest. Religion had an everyday influence over the Utilians. Both the women and men worked very hard and it was all manual labor.

Dinner (lunch) was always at noon. This was a time when the whole family would gather together like clockwork. We meet at home and would sit around the dinner table no matter where we were or what we were doing at 12 p.m.

We the children had lots of flexibility. All we had was school and chores. The generation before us worked hard and each one before them worked even harder. We the children of the sixties were born at a time that when change was beginning to come to the island.

Our kerosene lantern was still burning low on the kitchen table when my father blew it out. The lampshade was dark with black soot. My mother lit the wood stove from the dried limbs and sticks that I had gathered during the day.

I began to smell the scents of fresh coffee, fried green bananas and fried pork.

The first rays of the morning sun slowly lit up the horizon to the east with an orange and yellow glow and entered my window. Another day had come once again to our little island. My father was at the kitchen table eating breakfast when I walked by in my underwear. "Good morning" we said to each other. We called him "dadad" and we called our mother "mommie".

My father, like many other men of Utila, was about to set out to farm his piece of land. He farmed when he was not working as a merchant seaman. Times got tough for us financially when he was not at sea. He would work for periods of 6 months to about a year and would come home for periods of one month to 6 months at a time depending on when they needed him. When he was working at sea, things were very good for our family.

He grew plantains, coconuts, pears (avocados) cassava (yuca), and whatever he could to make ends meet. He owned a big piece of land near

Pumpkin Hill Beach. After picking his fruits and vegetables he would bring them home to eat and some to sell. My sister and me would go door-to-door selling bananas at five cents a hand (6 to 8 bananas) and plantains for a "cinquito" (2 1/2 cents) each. We also sold pears (avocados) and picked crabmeat. We sold a lot door-to-door when my father was not at sea.

We would also put our fruits or vegetables in one of the shops to sell on consignment. Usually it was at Mr. Archie's shop. We would take pears (avocados), bananas, plantains and sometimes "cassava" (yuca) to Mr. Archie Henderson and get credit in his store. My parents would always say, "Mr. Archie was fair and always tried to cut someone a break". He would give us credit when times were tough and would not pressure my parents for payment.

I never liked selling anything. My sister sure did and would end up selling most of what I did not sell. I went to wash my face and brush my teeth. I poured some water from the barrel into a small basin. As I dipped my toothbrush in my plastic glass of water, I looked up through the window and saw a beautiful black and red bird. It was small and just sat there on a mango tree limb. All the feathers on the top of its head and down its back were a dark black, and all the feathers on its underbelly were red. We gathered around the kitchen table and started to eat breakfast.

Looking out the back door I saw a couple of people from the Point and Sandy Bay with their buckets and flashlights looking for mangoes. It was still early in the morning. Like a ritual the people would come to the Hill to pick up ripe mangoes that dropped during the night. They came before the sun rose. We had such a big concentration of the trees on the Hill that there was enough for everyone.

They had few to no mango trees on the Point and not as many in Sandy Bay as we did on The Hill so sooner or later everyone came to the Hill for ripe mangoes, children and adults. You would see people with a flashlight in one hand and a bucket or dishpan in the other hand picking up mangoes by to take home and eat or to make mango jam. Many nights, families or friends would sit on the steps with a bucket of mangoes and eat until our stomachs were full.

After eating so many at one time our faces and hands would be covered by the sticky but sweet juice. Some mornings looking out my window, all I could see was what looked like hundreds of individual flashlights under the trees. My father said he would be going to Puerto Cortes soon to catch s ship.

He would send or bring us boxes of "goodies" from the States. Me and my sisters, and quite a few other children were fortunate enough to have a father working at sea.

My father said goodbye to us, got on his horse Black Beauty, and set off to begin another day of work on his piece of land. I had asked my parents if I could get a bicycle the next time "dadad" went away to work and they said yes. My sister also gave my father a verbal list of the things she wanted him to bring her from the States. My parents would always find a way to get us what we wanted when we were growing up. A few minutes later, I saw Worman (Whitefield), picking up some of the best mangoes on the ground in the back of our house and I said hello. His bucket was almost full.

"Some good ones fell last night" he called out. "Yeah" I answered him. He was around the same age as me and lived on The Point with his parents Mr. Sheldon and Ms. Eva Whitefield along with his other brothers and sisters Delaney, Dillion, Dorcas, Kirk, Hoover, Sharon and Mardell. Worman was a little bit "crazy", like Wardo and Horace and a good all around athlete.

Out the window I saw Harold James "backing" (carrying) water from the public well up to his house, filling up their barrels. Like most people who did this, he used a long stick over his shoulders with a five-gallon can of water on each side hanging by a rope connected to the ends of the stick. He was huffing, puffing and sweating. Almost everyone on the island had one or two fresh water barrels, which were filled either by the rain or trips to the public well.

This water was used for everything and you understood it was limited. When it came to food and water, our parents would always say, "waste not, want not". All the water you had was what was in the barrels and you did not want them to go dry, especially at night. Except for those who had their own wells, everyone had a limited supply and if their barrels ran dry it was a major inconvenience.

If you lived on the low part of the town you hired someone with a wheelbarrow to roll barrels of water to your house. If you lived on the hilly part of the island you had to carry it by hand or by using a stick over your shoulders. The cost for filling a barrel was .25 cents. That was a lot of work but twenty-five cents was also a lot of money at that time.

Before eating breakfast, my mother asked me to run and buy a pint of milk. She gave me five cents and I walked next door to Mr. Leonidas back porch to buy the milk. But today he did not have any, or it had not yet arrived, so I walked up a little further to Ms. Chloe Morgan's house. She lived in a big house on the Hill with her husband Mr. Spencer Morgan and their children Frank and Martha. As I got near her house I noticed Mr. Jose Gomez walking along the side of his two-story house, which was next door. He was once the Chief of Police and lived at the top of the rocky road.

I went in through the gate of her yard up the back steps. "Good morning son" Ms. Chloe said. I gave her the nickel and handed her my plastic bottle. You had to take your own container when you went to buy milk. In fact you had to take your own containers whenever you bought any liquid: milk, kerosene, Clorox, gasoline, distillate, or vinegar.

I took the milk home and my mother emptied it in a small pot and put it on the stove to boil. We always boiled all our fresh milk and to a lesser extent our water. I sat down for breakfast. My sister took a slice of bread and dunked it in her coffee then took a bite. We all liked to dunk our bread first in the coffee before eating it. Some people just drank sweetened water instead of coffee.

After eating, I put on a pair of shorts and an old t-shirt. Then I and went barefoot under the house to look for Shaggy. All homes on the island were built on posts (stilts) measuring anywhere from about four feet to about 8 feet tall. Our house was about seven to ten feet off the ground. I found Shaggy lying down and called out to him. "Hey boy" I said as I petted him on his head. "Ya ready to go huntin'?" I asked. I gave him leftovers from breakfast and filled his bowl with fresh water for him to drink before we left.

My cousin Gilly (Harley Gillian Gregory) was next door with Gram (our grandmother), eating breakfast. I called out to him. "Ya still going?" He was sitting by the table. "No, I can't go" he answered. I was now ready to go hunting for iguanas because even if Gilly wasn't going, I knew I had to go. I picked up a mango and set off walking with Shaggy right behind, to meet up with my cousin Wardo (Edward McKenzie) who also said he would go hunting with us.

As I was leaving, I saw my mother go to the chicken coop to let out the chickens and our rooster so they could scavenge around for food in the yard. She would stand at the door of the coop and let the hens out, one at a time. My mother would check each one to see if they were to lay an egg that day. If any hens were to lay an egg, they would be put back into the coop and locked up. The rosters were always set free.

To figure out if a hen was to lay an egg, my mother, and the other women on the island, would stick her pinky finger into the hen's rectum and feel inside the chicken for an egg. If she felt an egg forming inside, then that hen would be put back into the coop for the day. Sometimes hens were let out without checking and they would lay their eggs in other people's yards. The women tried to avoid this as any eggs not in the coop could be lost to someone or eaten by an animal. Chickens would eat almost anything. They were always pecking, scratching the ground and picking, eating whatever they could find.

In fact, they ate more than pigs for their

size. During the day they would roam around all over the Hill searching for anything, including worms, fruits, vegetables, ants, and whatever else they could find to eat. When we could afford it we would buy corn (kernels) and throw it to the ground for them to eat. It helped them grow faster.

Setting off on my hunt, I walked down past Mr. Will and Ms. Norma Hinds house and said hello to Ms. Norma, who was washing dishes in her kitchen. She and Mr. Will lived there with their children Ann, Bill, Dave, Tony, Normita (Norma), Johnny, Debra and Merrill.

On the other side of the unpaved Cola (de) Mico Road from Mr. Will lived Mr. George Gabourel and his wife Ms. Iris. They had 8 children: Frank, Georgie (George), Jimmy, Linda, Edna, Helen, Oscar and Doris Ann. There was a "monkey cap" fruit tree in their front yard and I saw two, which had fallen to the ground. I picked them up.

When ripe, "monkey caps" were yellow and about 2 to 3 inches long, shaped like a small carrot with soft sweet meat and most of the fruit was made up of its seed.   Mr. George Gabourel had plenty of land. He also had cows and horses.   He also sold fresh cow milk and had a big horse called Trigger. "Budda" (Coburn) used to work for Mr. George Gabourel and was one of the few men that rode Trigger, who we considered to be a "bad" horse.

I then passed Mr. Milio (Emilio) Castillo and his wife Ms. Getty's house on the right. Their children were Penny, Avon, Girt Lee (Gertis), Joe Murray and Tammy Sue.   I believe Mr. Nado (Ms. Getty's father) owned the house and they all lived there together.

Mr. Nado was an old blind man and was a great storyteller. The children would gather around him many nights sitting on a bench in front of his house and listen to the many tales he would spin. Each story was as unbelievable as the next. He told us wild stories like the time he was in Alaska. It got so cold, he said, that when he would spit, it would turn to ice before hitting the ground. He said it would just freeze in midair and stay there.   Who were we to dispute

Mr. Nado? We knew nothing about Alaska, the cold weather or the outside world. As a child I believed most of his stories, as did most of the children.

On the left I passed the old Indian public well. Almost everyone relied on this well for his or her water. Many people were around the three-foot tall cement wall of the well. I saw Tim McCoy filling his barrel, which was standing upright on his wheelbarrow.

The men threw their buckets, tied with a rope, down into the well and pulled them up full of water. They would use this water to fill up five-gallon cans and/or barrels in wheelbarrow. The water from the well was clear and it tasted fresh. It was an art to throwing down your bucket, making it tilt at the last second to scoop up a full bucket and pull it up in almost one motion.

The well was about 15 to 20 feet deep, 8 to ten feet wide. The local Indians built it many years before the Spanish and the English came to the island. I walked a little further up Cola (de) Mico (Monkey Tail) Road until I reached the beginning of Lozano Road.

I passed Mr. Albert Gregory's house on the right and Mr. Baudich and Ms. Beatrice Bush's house on the left. Mr. Baudich and Ms. Beatrice lived there with their children Barbara, Yolanda, Edgar, Nanette, Ellie and Clara. Mr. Baudich brothers and sister were Tonce (Terrance), Eduardo, and Avani.

Mr. Albert and his wife Ms. Miriam had 2 children: Morris and Rudolph. Ms. Miriam also had Lolita, Adriana, Edith, Adeline and Calvin.

I made a left and went up Lozano Road to go to Wardo's house. The sun was shining without a cloud in the sky. I saw Mr. Baudich in his yard talking to Ms. Beatrice standing under their big breadfruit tree. As I got closer to aunt Irene's house, I heard uncle Joe (Joseph McKenzie) yelling and I walked carefully until I got in front of their yard.

I passed my aunt Carmen in the street. She had two children: Fred Aster Gregory and Joseph Angus. Uncle Joseph McKenzie was my father's half brother. Uncle Joe's father was Adorn McKenzie and he had three uncles living in Roatan: Clifton, Nathan and another who lived up the islands.

I saw Wardo sitting on the ground by the fresh water pump in the front yard. The area around the pump was filled in with white sand from the beach. The hand pump was connected to their well and they got their water from it each day. Many people in Savah would go to uncle Joe's pump for all their water. It was one that looked like those in the old western movies. You pumped the long handle up and down to make the water come up.

Wardo's legs were locked in a set of wooden stalks with a padlock. He was being punished, again. When he was bad, which was often, he would get a beating from uncle Joe and sometimes put in stalks so he would not be able to go anywhere, and today was one of those days.

Wardo was one of those children who were not afraid of anything or anyone and always willing to press his luck. Dogs were afraid of him. He fought more times that he could remember. Thank God he was my double first cousin and we got along well. My father and his father were brothers; his mother and my mother were sisters.

I said hello to Aunt Irene, who was under the house floor cooking on her old wood stove. One of their dogs was lying on the ground next to back of the stove. "Good morning son" she said to me. Their kitchen was in the open under their house floor at that time. I asked Wardo what happened. He was sobbing and his words just could not come out clear. Uncle Joseph stepped in and said "Go where you goin' but he ain't goin' huntin".

"Joseph, let the boy go hunting" aunt Irene called out from under the house. Uncle Joe would not change his mind. With Shaggy by my side I started walking up Lozano Road and at the same time I saw the boys coming towards me. I said bye to Wardo.

Clinty was with Hobart and Andrew Bernard and another boy. They were 4 to 6 years older than me. They had 2 dogs. Hobart and Andrew were the sons of Mr. Thomas and Ms. Annie Bernard, and lived up Lozano Road with their other brother Augustus and their sisters Minnie Rose, Joanie, Barbara, Dawn, Eunice and June.

Clinty lived out in town next to Ms. May Woods with his mother Ms. Lyna, his grandmother Ms. Lottie and his brother Leroy. "Could I go with you?" I asked to neither one in particular. "Yeah, just don't get in our way" Hobart said. Even though they told me the day before that I could go, I just wanted to be sure.

I followed them back down Lozano Road until we got to the end where Mr. Baudich Bush and Mr. Albert Gregory lived across from each other.

We made a left and headed into the bush, where we were joined by a couple of other boys. The sun was now very hot. Every boy was barefoot. We passed Mr. Marshall Zelaya's house. He had a very big piece of land. It was so big in fact, that we played baseball in his front yard almost every week at times. He lived there with his wife Ms. Jenny and young Marshall and Jenny Lee. Their other children were Rafael, Trina, Reynaldo and Miguel.

The ground was getting hot and made the dirt road heat up the bottoms of our dusty feet. Hobart had a long stick with a thin rope tied into a noose, at one end. It was used for catching iguanas, which we also referred to as guanas, hammos and wishiwillies.

My dog Shaggy walked behind us with the other dogs as we passed aunt Victoria's (Bolan) house. She lived on the left with her husband uncle Percy Bolan and their children Shirley and Oscar. After you passed Aunt Victoria's house, you were in the bush from that point on.

We stopped to pick some plums from a big tree on the right. We had Spanish and hog plums. The trees were plentiful but you had to be careful because like most ripe fruits on the island, many had small worms. Most people would have to take some form of medicine to clean out their system, a couple times during the year from eating so many "wormy" fruits. We would drink "seena" and other bush medicines, which worked really well. Usually it was a drink made from the roots or leaves of plants. Home remedies were a big part of our lives on the island.

We finished picking up plums and headed off confident, feeling that we would catch a few iguanas. "Ah bet we gah catch a lot of wishiwillies," Clinty said. Everybody nodded in agreement.

Further up ahead we stopped and Clinty climbed a "hog" plum tree. The fruits were about a half-inch round and an inch long. When I looked up, I saw hundreds of bunches of plums ranging in colors from green to yellow. Most hog plums were sweet as sugar when ripe, even though most of the fruit was made up of its' seed. The trees were tall and the plums were plentiful. Every limb had many bunches.

Clinty climbed one tree and positioned himself on a limb where he was surrounded by bunches and bunches of ripe hog plums. He sat there on the limb picking and eating the plums when Hobart called up to him "Throw us some, don't be so hoggish (greedy)". Clinty laughed out loud and spit out a seed at Hobart, then picked a few bunches and threw them down to us. The juice was sweet, especially on a hot day like today. It rolled down the sides of my mouth.

After about fifteen minutes of eating plums our stomachs were full and we moved on ahead on our hunt. I trailed behind the older boys. We reached Mr. Hanford Bodden's grass piece (pasture) where he kept his cows. He was just coming out from the cow pen, bending between the second and third rows of barbed wire that surrounded his land. "What are you boys up to today? Mr. Hanford asked in his deep voice. "Goin' huntin' Mr. Hanford" Clinty said.

Mr. Hanford was married to Ms. Elyse and they lived out in the part of town we called Holland with their children Vivian Anne, Delmar, Donna, Steve, Raul, Olive, Sandra, Duke Snyder and Hodgers.

Mr. Hanford was once the mayor of Utila and he was also the captain of several freight/passenger boats that made trips back and forth from the island to the mainland. He owned a lot of land in the bush. He was a tall man with light brown skin. He and Ms. Elyse also owned a grocery shop and sometimes sold cooked food.

He was sweating and took a piece of cloth from his back pocket and wiped his face. The sun was now really beating down on the island, but this was normal Utila weather.

"When you gonna kill a cow?" Clinty asked him. "Next Saturday" Mr. Hanford replied as he reached out and took a couple of hog plums from a bunch Hobart was holding in his hand. He put one in his mouth and you could see by his eyes that the hog plum was sweet. He smiled and walked away.

At this point my dog Shaggy saw the cows in the pen and took off under the barbed wire running after them. The cows did not run but he kept on barking as he ran deeper into the grass piece to bark at another group of cows. I yelled at Saggy but he just kept on running and did not return. "That's some huntin' dog." Clinty said. Everybody laughed. That was not the way I wanted this hunting trip to begin.

We continued walking and I kept looking back to see if maybe Shaggy would catch up with us. He never did. Just a few minutes later, Clinty motioned with his hand for us to stop. He then put his finger to his mouth signaling the rest of us to be quiet. He saw an iguana on a limb of a tree to the right of the road. We could see the silhouetted body of the iguana on the limb against the morning sun to the east. We put our hands over our eyes to block the sun as we looked up. I saw it sitting there alone, not moving.

Clinty climbed the tree by pushing himself up with his bare feet and pulling his body up with his arms until he got to the limbs. He got up the tree pretty fast and he was quiet. The excitement within me grew stronger by the seconds. He pointed to the 5-foot iguana sitting out on the limb catching sun. Iguanas set aside hours each day to sit in the sun, so we looked on tree limbs and cliff rocks.

Clinty reached down and motioned for the stick with the noose and Hobart handed it to him. We were all quiet. I heard a blackbird "squawk" in the distance.

Hobart and Andrew positioned themselves and the rest of us to stand under the iguana. Clinty pulled the noose open and held the stick by the other end in his right hand. He got as close as he could without startling the animal. But if the iguana jumped, which they often did, the rest of us were waiting for it below. Some had sticks that would be used to hit the iguana if it dropped or jumped from the limb.

When Clinty got close enough to the iguana, he took the stick by the end and slowly reached out to position the noose above the iguana's head without making a sound. Clinty was sweating a lot as he sat out on the limb moving quietly. When the noose was close over the iguana's head, he quickly slipped it over its neck and jerked it. He hooked the iguana, which now was dangling by the noose.

The iguana whipped and swung its tail, struggling to get free. It was now fighting for its life. Clinty pulled the stick in and grabbed the iguana by its head with one hand and its tail with the other hand while leaning against the trunk of the tree, standing on a limb. The iguana now had little to no chance of survival.

The rope and stick hung from the iguana's neck as Clinty loosened the noose. You had to be careful and keep the iguana from biting you or swiping you with its tail. "Bring him down" called out Hobart. "Give him to me." Andrew said to Clinty.

You could hear the individual drops of sweat falling from Clinty's body as each one hit the dry leaves on the ground. His arm was bulging with muscles testifying to the strength with which he was holding the iguana. There was no way this iguana would escape. Today would be his last.

Clinty let go of the iguana's tail for a quick second and put his left hand up around the iguana's neck to join the right hand. He twisted the iguana's neck with one snap. The iguana flapped its tail and it was now dead.

Clinty gave the stick to Hobart and slowly came down from the tree. "That's a big one" I said, "let's go catch some more". Andrew said.
"Wanna hold him" Hobart asked me. I said yes. I took the iguana and held by its neck with my two

hands.   I did not want to take a chance the iguana was not dead and was scared. I did not want him to bite me. We continued walking for about fifteen minutes.

It was a beautiful day and the birds were singing.

Not too far ahead, Hobart saw another iguana and pointed it out to the rest of us.   This one was far up the tree and out on a small limb.   It would be very difficult to reach this one by climbing the tree. Hobart and Clinty directed all of us to pick up rocks.   At his signal all of us began throwing them at the iguana, trying to knock it off the limb. The dogs were barking with excitement. The iguana was startled and held its head up to about a 45-degree angle to investigate.

The dogs understood this was a hunt and the iguana knew it was the hunted. I just wished my dog Shaggy had not run away.   Suddenly a rock thrown by Hobart hit the iguana and it fell to the ground and without missing a beat, took off running. It fled into the grassland with the dogs and all of us boys in close pursuit.

I followed behind the others, as I could not run too fast while holding the dead iguana in my hands. Running barefoot through thick bushes could be tricky, as you never knew what was beneath just waiting to stick you in your feet. There were prickles (thorns), pointed sticks, rocks and so much more you had to think about. Going barefoot all the time, everyone got their share of nails, glass, splinters or prickles stuck in their feet at one time or the other.

The dogs led the way and the iguana was now in a run for its life. It seemed like an eternity but it was only about one minute when the dogs lost the iguana and stopped running but continued barking under a tree.

It seemed the iguana ran up a big pear (avocado) tree but no one could be sure, as we could not see it. The dogs were not 100% sure either. After looking up the tree for a couple of minutes we decided we lost this one and moved on ahead, retracing our way back. We came to some grass that would cut you like a knife. It was razor sharp and it cut a few of us.

Suddenly the dogs turned around and started running back while barking out loud. It seems the iguana was game again as it left its hiding place and ran through the dried leaves. The iguana was in a desperate attempt to escape but the dogs were right behind it

Today, it was in the wrong place at the wrong time. The animal must have been terrified, I thought as I ran behind. I gave the dead iguana I was holding to another boy as I struggled to keep up. The dogs followed the iguana closely and we followed the dogs.

We caught up and found one of the dogs with the iguana in its mouth holding it securely with its teeth around the neck. Clinty tried to remove the iguana. The dog growled and did not want to give up its catch. Finally, Hobart managed to pry the dog' mouth open and remove the iguana.

We walked back to the main road. I felt good, like I had caught an iguana myself. We passed Mr. Ed Rubi who was walking ahead of his horse coming out of the bush. Mr. Rubi lived on the Point.

His father was Mr. "Gavino" and his mother was Ms. Lupe Rubi. Their children were Louis, Charlie, Nellie Jean, Vinnie and Sarah.

"I see you caught a couple," Mr. Ed Rubi said as he passed us going in the opposite direction. His horse was loaded with 4 sacks of coconuts. Like many on the island, his mare made the same exact trip every day for years and knew by memory where their owners lived and where they farmed.

The sun was now very hot, even for Utila, as we walked in line one after the other up the road. Clinty advised us all he had to "dee-tee" so he went into the bushes behind a tree. As there were no toilets you went in the bushes to "pee pee or dee tee". You would just find yourself a "secluded" area and did your duty. Clinty went under a plum tree. As the rest of us waited for him, we picked up some hog plums, which had dropped to the ground. Their juice lit up my mouth with a sweet burst as I bit into the fruits.

There were some guava trees to the left of the road and there were ripe bananas hanging from trees on the right of us. We picked some of each and ate them. It was a beautiful day.

There were fruit trees all around, no matter where you found yourself on the island. I saw a couple of blackbirds flying around the top of the plum trees. Clinty finally came out from the bushes and he was pulling up his short pants.

After walking another fifteen minutes, we caught a couple more iguanas for a total of four or five. We decided to head back home. Judging by the position of the sun, it was getting close to midday. We used the sun very well in telling time as so very few of us had watches.

The bigger boys began sharing up the iguanas. But I went home empty handed. One of these days I would be big enough to share in the catch. Hobart and Andrew told me to come around later and they would give me some cooked iguana.

We stopped by my Aunt Victoria's house on our way out and asked her for some water. She used a tall yellow plastic glass and filled it from the barrel and passed it to one us. The dogs drank from a pan of water under the house that Aunt

Victoria had for her dog. Each one drank some water and passed the glass to the next boy and Aunt Victoria kept refilling the glass. We were thirsty.

On her clothesline I could see that she washed her white clothes that morning. She had all her sheets and towels hung out on the lines to dry. After washing them by hand on a washboard, the women would put all the white clothes in a metal tub and boil them. They stirred the clothes with a long paddle. Not only did the men work hard at that time, so did the women. They would add a marble sized ball of "blue", which evaporated in the hot water.

They said the "blue" made everything whiter. The women would be in the hot sun, with a white piece of cloth tied around their heads, hanging out their clothes to dry. When I reached home, my mother asked me to go to the shop and buy some things she would need for supper. We had breakfast, dinner and supper. We knew nothing about lunch.

She gave me a quarter and asked me to buy three

cents coffee, 2 breads at five cents each, (the small ones were three-cents each), 3 cents sugar and 2 cents worth of salt. "Bring back the change" she called out as I headed down the hill past Ms. Julia's house.

I quickly arrived at Mr. Dempsey Thompson's small shop and waited to be served, as he was busy talking to his wife, Ms. Hester. All the women over a certain age were referred to as Ms. instead of Mrs. whether they were married or not.

"Good morning son, what can I get you?" asked Mr. Dempsey. I called out my list as I remembered it and he started to get the items. I heard a hen "cackling" in the yard and I looked out the window to see that a rooster was chasing it.

Mr. Dempsey's roots went back to England or Ireland. He was well spoken on worldly topics, so it was always interesting to go to his shop. He and Ms. Hester had eight daughters: Sharon Stephanie, Debbie, Winifred, Annie, Gayle, Ollie, Scarlett and Janice Hope and they lived in their house which was right next to the shop.

While waiting, I saw Elden Bush standing in the road in front of his house, which was next door to Mr. Dempsey's shop. "Is your "pappa" goin' kill a pig today?" I asked. "Yes" he answered. He was untangling his fishing line, which was tied around a small Clorox bottle. We knew nothing about rods and reels. It was all by hand.

We never used mother or father when talking about each other's parents. It was always his "mamma" or her "pappa." And it was said in a slow accented drawl. Across the street from Mr. Dempsey lived Ms. May Woods, her mother was Ms. Ezemina and her children were Sheila and Julio. She also had a brother "Hijo" (Cuffbert Woods) who lived in the same house.

Through the opened back door, I saw Ms. May Woods who ran a restaurant/bakery, open her oven door. She baked great tasting cakes, pies and shortcakes.

I picked up the items from the counter and headed home. I made sure I had everything and I put the change in my pocket.

The unpaved street was hot as my bare feet

touched the road on my way back home. I passed Elden who lived in the house with his parents Mr. Spurgeon and Ms. Pansy (Hinds) Bush. His brother and sisters were Halcyan, James Ray, Edith, Janet, and Evelyn.

In the road were a group of black rocks buried in the ground but sticking out about two inches. I "bucked" my toe on one of them and yelled out in pain. I walked home limping with the groceries, thinking about eating "chicharon" (pigskin) later that day when Mr. Spurgeon killed the pig.

As I came up the hill, I passed Mr. Louie and Ms. Violet McField's house. They had 3 children: Stanford, Reina and Inda. On the right lived Mr. Nulfo Ramos and his wife Ms. Sara and their children Irma and Ramon.

On the side of the road, Mr. Louie had a short "soupa" tree. They were round hard fruits about an inch in diameter, like a big marble, with a thin but hard plastic-like skin covering them. The "soupas" were protected by many long black "prickles" (thorns), which grew out from the trunk of the tree.   The prickles were about three to five inches long and were intimidating. You did not want any part of your body to touch the tree.   I guess that was how the tree protected its fruits.

You had to be very careful running down this road to not run into the soupa tree. My brother Carlos (Charles Longsworth) did just that once when he visited us. Running down the winding road he could not turn fast enough and ran right into the soupa tree. He had thorns stuck into his body and they were deep. The wounds looked ugly must have been painful.

As I got closer to our house, I passed Ms. Julia James' house. She lived right next to us with her children Harold and Tina. I saw my dog Shaggy coming running towards me. "Wha" happened to you boy?" I asked him as I knelt down to hug him while holding some groceries in each hand.

I loved my dog Shaggy and was happy to see him. "You ran away, bad boy." I said as we came into our yard. There were ripe mangoes all over the ground. Ms. Julia had a big "cut short" mango tree in her yard and the tree dropped so many that they covered the yard.

I took the groceries, which were all put into small brown paper bags or paper funnels and put them in the kitchen on the table and went outside to play. My mother was talking to Ms. Nessie, who lived in front of us with her husband Mr. Alfred Ponce.   They had 6 children: Janet, Kenneth, Lola, Karen, Sophia, and Desiree.

My mother and Ms. Nessie were talking while my sister Lola and Janet played nearby. Suddenly my sister and Janet got into a fight. It seems that Janet told my sister her birthday was July 11, and my sister thinking only one person could have the same birth date challenged Janet over whose birth date it was on July 11th, and they fought. I think there was blood.

After separating the two, my mother tried to explain to my sister that two people could have the same birth date. My sister, two years younger than me would need a little longer to fully understand that concept. She stuck to her belief that it was only her birthday on July 11

They settled down and began to play again in the sand. I climbed the "cannup" tree in Ms. Nessie's yard. Cannups were small green fruits about the size of a marble. It was made up mostly of seed but had a thin layer of "meat" that was sweet. This tree always had a lot of sweet fruits on its limbs and this season it was flourishing.

There could be anywhere from four to twenty cannups on a bunch and each limb had many bunches. I climbed up to about ten feet off the ground and picked all the cannups I could reach. I ate so many my stomach began to hurt. Then I ate more, spitting out the skin and leaving the seed in my mouth. Cannup juice would stain your clothes on contact and I got its juice all over my clothes.

I went looking for Gilly and found him on Gram's porch eating a piece of bread. "Wanna go to see if they're cooking the wishiwillies?" I asked him. "Ok" Gilly said and we walked down the Hill through the back. We passed under a big marmey tree and saw that a couple of them had dropped from the tree. We each picked up one. They were delicious fruits. They had a brown skin and orange colored meat.

We went down to Uncle Joseph and Aunt Irene McKenzie's house. They lived there with their children Wardo (Edward), Joe Louis, Margaret, Richard, Harry Truman, Elsa Lee, Betty, and Lorna.

Wardo was under the house where the kitchen was located. Aunt Irene was at the wood stove cooking. She was short and skinny, with light skin. She always would give you a cheerful hello and ask you how you were doing. Uncle Joe had let Wardo out from his punishment and the three of us walked up Lozano road to see how the cleaning of the wishiwillies was coming along. On their steps we saw Hobart, Andrew and Augustus along with Clinty.

Hobart laid the dead iguana on its back while sitting on the steps. He then took his sharp knife and cut the iguana's stomach from the mouth to the beginning of its tail. He began to peel the thin leather like skin off the iguana with his hands. He ripped it off piece by piece, then reached into the dead iguana's stomach and pulled out all it's internal organs and threw them to the dogs as a reward. He put the iguana's eggs in a bowl, as these were a delicacy. Clinty was also cleaning an iguana.

"We need some salt and black "peppa" Hobart said. He asked us to go buy some. He gave us four cents and we went up the road to the left to Mr. John "Bull" Bodden's shop.

When we got there, I asked Mr. John "Bull" for 2 cents salt and 2 cents black "peppa". He lived there with his wife Ms. Annie. They had seven children: Selwyn, Hester, Leila, Bill, Johnny, Carol, Henry, Osten, and Nanny "Bull". In addition to his shop, he also owned cows and he farmed.

His daughter Ms. Nanny "Bull" had a ham radio and whenever there was an emergency and someone had to be contacted while away, people would go to her to "call" the States. We had no phones on the island, except for one Mr. Frank Morgan and his mother Ms. Chloe had a black wall phone in their shop. I think it was connected directly to their house up on The Hill if it was working.

We took the salt and black pepper back and they had just begun to cut up the iguanas into pieces to be cooked. In the next yard I saw Ms. Trixie. She was standing with her husband Mr. William Buckley outside their house.

They lived there with their children Rosie, Cherry Ann, Dewey, Davis, Carol, Cora, Claris May, Janelle, Grace, Amy Hope, Tom, Tony and Marjorie. She was a powerful brown skinned-woman who was strong and feared no one.

They had a barrel on the side of their house, which collected rainwater and was standing next to it talking to Mr. William Buckley. Someone had put some dirt and or bushes in the water and now they had to empty it, clean it and refill it. They were not happy. They called their son Dewey out from the house and told him to wash out the barrel and "back" water from my uncle Joseph's well to fill it again. Dewey was also not happy and let out a few choice words. In the pot with the meat they also put in the iguana eggs. They had a chewy inside with a thin white skin.

"Can I have some cooked eggs?" Wardo asked. "Come back later and you'll get a taste," Augustus said to us. The dogs were barking and fighting each other for the iguana's remains thrown to the ground. While they fought, a small black cat swooped in and grabbed a piece in its mouth and sped off to eat it.

Me, Gilly and Wardo headed back down Lozano Road. "They ga (going to) kill pig today" I said to the two of them. "Mr. Spurgeon?" asked Gilly. "Yeah" I replied. "Let's go see em' kill him," one of us said.

We turned right and headed out town towards Mr. Spurgeon's house. Gilly said hello to his grandfather Mr. Albert Gregory who was sitting on his porch. We passed Mark Bush, who was heading off to do some farming with a sack and a "machett" (machete). Mark lived on the other side of Lozano Road, across the street from Ms. Trixie. He and Steve were sons of Ms. Della and Mr. Clayton Bush. Their brothers and sisters were Ruth, Esther, Onay, Frank, Dale, Harriet,

Olita, Parker and Tasha.

I could hear the pig making noise in the distance as we passed Mr. Calvin and Ms. Doreen Woods' house. Sounds traveled so far and clear on Utila at this time, as they were all natural, having no cars or other motors to cause interference.

Mr. Calvin and Ms. Doreen lived next door to Mr. Clifford and Ms. Emma Woods. Mr. Calvin and Ms. Doreen lived with their children Clyde (Boozie), Mehitible, Calvin (CJ), Darien, Murden (Buggy), Addis, and Sandy Kerry.

Ms. Emma and Mr. Clifford Woods children were Aaron, Enrique, Morris, Ivey and Lolo (Lolita). Soon we passed Mr. Georgie's house.

Mr. Spurgeon killed a pig almost every week, sometimes two times a week. He would fry out the pig's fat into lard and send it to the mainland to sell, where it fetched a good return. He would also sell the fried pigskin (chicharon) along with the liver and other internal organs. You could buy it by the pieces, or together with a piece of fried plantain or banana and call it a "con yuca" for five cents or ten cents depending on what extra you got. There was also a mix of cabbage and onions and vinegar that was put on your "con yuca."

I always tried to engage the pig's tail whenever I could, but it was difficult as Mr. Spurgeon's daughter Halcyan usually engaged it ahead of time. The tail cost 5 cents and tasted great. Each piece of chicharon "pigskin" cost cinquito or 2 1/2 cents. Me, and my sister would try to get five cents each from our mother, or father and buy a plate every time Mr. Spurgeon would kill a pig. My parents usually had enough to give us, especially when my father was working on the ships.

The weekly pig-killing event was brutal and a ritual. Even though I always felt sorry for the pig, I kept coming to Mr. Spurgeon's yard almost every week to see the killing and happily ate the pig's meat afterwards.

The men would gather around before the killing where they would talk, gossip and just to be part of the "fry out".

We got to Mr. Spurgeon's house and the preparations had already begun. There was a half drum of water boiling under a medium fire on an outdoor metal base. The half-drum was black with soot on the outside from the many times it was used. Mr. Spurgeon's son Elden would clean the inside after each fry out.

I saw Elden standing, holding a rope tied to the pig's neck. We went over to say hello. The sow was howling and putting up a fight but Elden kept a strong hold on the rope. The pig was black with white spots all over its body. It was hot and flies were beginning to gather. Chickens and dogs also gathered as if they knew what was about to happen. There would be food.

Holding the rope tied to the pig, Elden threw it over a limb of a tree. At this point they were ready for the kill. Elden pulled the rope tight and the pig had very limited movement. The idea was to get the pig's head in the right position to take a clear hard blow from the dull side of an ax, which was swung by Mr. Spurgeon or a man he selected. They always tried to use just one blow from the ax to bring down the pig as more than one was considered "cruel."

Mr. Spurgeon took his ax and walked to the pig's right side. Elden moved back and held the rope. Me, Wardo and Gilly also moved away, but our eyes were glued to the unfolding event. Everyone was now quiet and looking on. Mr. Spurgeon slowly raised the ax above his head with his two outstretched arms. "Hold "im" good" he said to Elden.

Mr. Spurgeon brought the ax down with the speed and power of a home run hitter. There was a brutal thud and screams from the pig as the back of the ax connected to its forehead.

The pig dropped to the ground almost instantly into what looked like an epileptic attack, jerking and making a loud screeching high-pitched sound as it grasped its last breaths of air. Mr. Spurgeon took a long, sharp butcher's knife and bent over the pig's head and cut its throat from side to side. The blood gushed out and drained like a dark red river in the dry sand. It flowed out into several directions. The flies moved in and went for the blood. They were followed by the chickens and then by the dogs. The pig's body was still shaking and moving as they hoisted it by a rope tied to each hind leg and thrown over the tree limb. It was hanging head down.

Small pots of hot water would be thrown on its skin to loosen up the hairs on its body. A man on each side would then begin "shaving" off the hairs on the pig with their sharp knives. There would be about six or seven people at first but the crowd grew steadily.

Once the pig was scrapped clean of the hairs, Mr. Spurgeon took his knife and cut the stomach open from its tails up to its neck with one long straight cut. There would be a tub under the pig's head waiting to collect the organs of the pig. The heart, the "lites", the guts (intestines), were all cut out and separated. Very few pieces were ever thrown away.

The smallest pieces of fat and whatever little meat that was left over could be sold to people as scraps. They would in turn fry these pieces for their family or cooked and re-sold at three to five cents a piece along with a piece of fried green plantain, banana or chata.

The insides removed, Mr. Spurgeon would cut off the pig's skin in long slabs about four to five inches wide and the length of the pig. These slabs would be thrown on a table and cut in pieces of about five to six inches long, our "chicharon."

After throwing out or using all the hot water, pieces of skin and pieces of fat were thrown into the half drum. You could see the fat begin to melt and now it was boiling hot oil. Mr. Spurgeon directed someone to stir the pot. A man took a long dory paddle and began to stir the meat in the fryer. It was an art to cook pigskin just right so it would come out crispy. Now the skin, the organs and the bananas were coming to a hot boil. Mr. Spurgeon sprinkled some water over the boiling skin and it made a crackling sound. It sent smoke up from the fryer. He then sprinkled some salt over the fry as they continued stirring the contents of the pot.

I saw Wanda James and her cousin Halcyan

talking on the other side of the yard. "Ma pet" the tail is for me," Halcyan said to Wanda, who was the daughter of Mr. Tony and Ms. Grace (Hinds) James and her sister was Tonia. They lived out in Holland, next to Ms. Grace parents Mr. Sammy (Samuel) and Ms. Pansy Hinds.

Mr. Tony also had another daughter named Mary. Mr. Sammy and Ms. Pansy Hinds had 10 children: Oriella, Thomas, Earl, Mary, Elmer, Grace, Pansy, Erick, Stella and Maggie. Mr. Tony James parents were Mr. Van Wick and Ms. Rosa James. Their children were Stacey, Annie, Osgood, Jorgensen, Trixie, Carrie and Tony.

The fire under the fryer was blazing and Elden kept putting more dry limbs. It was frightening some times to see the brutality involved in the killing of a pig or cow, then surprising to see how much fun we had seeing the whole process.

The sounds, the smell, and the gruesomeness stayed with you. I ran home to get some money from my mother to buy some chicharon. You would use a leaf from the almond tree in Mr. Spurgeon's yard to hold the fresh and hot chicharon.

It cost a "cinquito" (2 ½ cents) for a piece of pigskin. You could also buy a piece of the heart, liver or "lites". Mr. Spurgeon would have a large bowl of vinegar, salt, pepper, and onions mixed and ready to pour with a tablespoon over your con yuca.

The skin of the intestines would be sold mostly on the mainland to people who would in turn use it to stuff with meat and sell as chorizos. I got to our house and asked for 5 cents from my mother who always said yes.

My sister Lola also got five cents. We ran back with our money securely held in our hands. I took my almond leaf and bought a piece of chicharon. But neither Wardo nor Gilly brought any money so I shared mine with them.

The pigskin was hot and we blew on it trying to cool it, but nether one of us had the time or patience to wait. I broke it into three pieces. It was a good "crackling" and crispy sound and the smell was great. I saw "Boozie" (Clyde Woods) in the front of the yard talking to Morris (Woods), his cousin, and went over to ask them about whether we would be playing baseball on in Mr. Marshall's yard.

"Ya ga (You're going to) play tomorrow?" I asked them. They knew I was talking about baseball. "Yeah" they both said almost at the same time. I saw Dewey (Buckley) laughing with his brother Davis in the road just outside Mr. Spurgeon's yard. They were about 7 to 10 older than me.

I went back and told Gilly and Wardo about playing baseball tomorrow. Gilly didn't want to play but Wardo was excited. I asked them to go with me to see if Hobart and Augustus had gotten the wishiwilly cooked.

We made our way up Lozano Road again and came to the front of Mr. Thomas Bernard's house. We saw Augustus and Andrew under their house and called out to them, asking if the wishiwillies were cooked. Augustus said it was almost finished and went inside and brought us a couple of pieces of the cooked iguana and a couple of eggs.

We sat on the front steps and ate all he

brought. It tasted so good, and whoever cooked it sure knew how to cook iguana. In my opinion, it's meat tasted like chicken but with its own unique bony texture. It was cooked with coconut milk, hot peppers and other seasonings. I think their mother Ms. Annie Bernard did the cooking. After eating the pieces they gave us, we headed out town, ending up by Mr. Spurgeon's house again. Most of the people at the killing were gone.

It was now about 6 p.m. and we saw Ms. Lilly Gay Ramon coming down the Rocky Road in front of Mr. Spurgeon's house with her bag of marbles. She was ready to play. Anytime any child wanted to play marbles or "chapas" (metal soda bottle caps), they only needed to go and find Ms. Lilly Gay.

She was on the larger side of a woman and dark-skinned. She was competitive and always wanted to win. We all ran home to get our marbles.

Ms. Lilly Gay always loved playing with the children and had no problem beating us and feeling good about it. She lived up the other

Rocky Road with her husband Mr. Joe (Joseph) Ramon and their daughter Selley.

We returned a little later with our marbles and began to play. It was now the season for marbles. We played almost every week. There was a bunch of us playing today: Gilly, myself, Wardo, Lola, Boozie, Morris, Charles Sanders, Clinty, and a few other boys and a couple girls.

Waiting to play or just watching was "Bullitt" Whitefield, Lindell, Freddie Gabourel, and a few others. "Bullit"s parents were Mr. "Dickie" and Ms. Mary Whitefield.

"Time to play" Ms. Lilly Gay said and we began. The games were intense, as nobody wanted to lose. I played until it was time to go home and I headed up the Hill with Gilly, Wardo and my sister Lola. I lost most of my marbles.

We passed Mr. Louie's "soupa" tree and shortly got to my house. Wardo and Gilly went home and my sister and I went inside. My father had just gotten back from farming and was eating. I saw he had 2 sacks of coconuts and a half sack of pears (avocados) lying on the ground by Black

Beauty. There was also a bunch of bananas, which had about seven "hands". Each hand had about six bananas. This meant me and my sister would have to go out selling tomorrow. I hated selling.

After eating, my father would sit down on the bed without his shirt and we would pick the ticks off him and kill them between the nails of our thumbs. While picking the ticks, he and my mother told us that he would be leaving next week to catch a ship.

While working out at sea, he would send or bring us many things from the States. Things like Corn Flakes, oatmeal, Cream of wheat, Diamond matches, Fruit Cocktail, canned peaches and always books, which I loved to read. My mother always encouraged us to read as many books as possible. Our lives were very good when my father worked on the ships. I washed up and got ready for bed. I had such a great day. I ate iguana, pigskin and played marbles.

Chapter Two

Weeks passed and the island was really hot. This particular week, it seemed like the heat rose before the sun, or like it just never left. If you had a cap you wore it, the ladies would never leave home without their umbrellas for protection against the sun.

Me, Gilly and Wardo had planned to go fishing down Sandy Bay. We would meet with our cousins Lee Lee (Leonard) and Tony Boy (Alfred) Ebanks. They were sons of my uncle Edward and aunt Mary Ann (Angus) Ebanks. They would later have 3 more boys: Joseph (Joe Joe), Sammy and Clyde (Kid Kay). Uncle Edward brothers and sisters were Alda Rose, Dorothy (Dolly Baby), Steven (Bud Bud), Beverly, Lemuel and Osten. Their parents were Ms. Sissy (Julia Ramon) and Mr. Asha Ebanks.

We planned to fish down by Mr. Bud Bud's house, which was built on posts that stood over the sea. The day before, we started getting everything ready so we would be able to leave early in the morning. Gilly, Wardo and me got together in

Gram's yard next to ours. We sat on a big black rock in her back yard and talked while we got our equipment together.

The fishing lines were rolled around a plastic bottle. After making sure our fishing lines were in order with hooks and sinkers, we talked about bait.

One of the best baits we used, were small animals we called "soldias". These were crustaceans in a white/grey/black colored spiral shell about one to two inches tall and wide. Some could be as big as three to four inches tall. Their bodies went around and up in their shells. Sticking out was the upper body that contained the eyes, head, claws, (bitters) and legs.

They would crawl around, mostly at night, on the ground searching for food. The lower half of the "soldias" bodies, in the tail end of the shell, was made up of a clear soft section, covered by a thin outer lining which when separated from the rest of the body would be put on your hook and used out as bait. The fish loved "soldias".

We would spread coconut "trash" (the remains of grated coconuts) on the ground around large tree roots and around large rocks. We knew the favorite spots where the animals looked for food.

Wardo said his "mamma" (mother) had saved him some coconut trash from the day before so we went down, over the back of the Hill to get it. We passed Ms. "BiBi's" house, which was located in the back of my grandmother Mannettie and grandfather Joseph Angus' house. Her children were Ivan, Ideel, Wade and Wayne. They had a beautiful house.

We passed a big marmey tree and picked up two of the fruits to take on our fishing trip. Next, we passed Ms. Romana's house on the right. Mr. Laurie Thompson and his wife Ms. Aurora's house was next door. His nieces Wanda Hope and Sherry Lyn also lived in the house.

The three of us walked barefoot in the bright hot sun talking about nothing in particular as we made our way down the road with bushes on each side. Birds were singing from almost every tree, and there were fruits all around. It was a beautiful day. The smell in the air was a potpourri of fruits. It was getting late in the afternoon and we had not long ago finished eating supper. In aunt Irene's front yard was a big "gumba limba" tree and it stood out with it's beautiful red leaves.

We saw Stevo (Steve Bush) with a sack on his back and sweating like a horse. Stevo stopped to show us some beautiful "pawpaws" (papayas) he had in his sack. The papayas were ripened just enough to eat. They were changing their color from green to yellow. Wardo asked him for one but Stevo said he could not give any of them away. "My "pappa" gonna sell them to someone." he said.

"We goin' fishin' tomoro'" Wardo said to Stevo. We called him muscle man. Stevo had more muscles than almost any child on the island. He got them mostly from hard work. Anywhere else in the world he would have been called a child body builder.

We waited until just before dark and set out to spread the coconut trash around the large roots of the many fruit trees and also around the big rocks up on the Hill. The "soldias" would be drawn to the smell of food and we would be waiting. Later that night we got a flashlight and a big "klim" pan and set off to find our bait. My dog Shaggy followed us as we started looking down by a big mango tree in our back yard. We saw one, then two and then another. They were really out in force this night, and they were big "soldias". They crawled slow, so once we saw them with the flashlight, they could not escape.

I remember hearing the "klunk" sound their shells made as we threw the first ones in the metal pan. When you spotted one crawling on the ground, all you had to do was touch its shell and it would stop crawling. They sensed danger and I guess they did this to try and fool predators into thinking there was no animal in the shell.

We moved further in the back of our house and came to a big "crabboo" tree. We picked up as many of the fruits as we could and put in our pockets. We would take them to eat tomorrow on our fishing trip. We had mangoes, marmies, crabboos and a couple of ripe bananas to take with us. Nature always looked out for everyone on Utila. There were always an abundance of fruits no matter the month of the year. We stopped to talk to Kenton who lived on the Hill with his sister Glessie with their parents Mr. Checkwood and Ms. Edna Hill.

Mr. Jose his wife Ms. Annie Gomez and their children Rolando and Rose Marie lived on the other side by Ms. Chloe and her husband Mr. Spencer Morgan whose children were Frank and Martha. They lived in a big house. My mother had worked for the Morgan family years earlier cleaning their house, cooking and doing chores.

I would sometimes go to Ms. Chloe's house to buy milk in the morning before breakfast. The milk was fresh from the cow and without refrigerators had to be finished within twenty-four hours or it would spoil. The Morgan family had plenty of land. They also had a shop and the ice factory. You could also buy fresh milk from Mr. Leonidas Bernard and Mr. George Gabourel.
We talked with Kenton for a while then set out to

catch more "soldias". We had two large tin cans almost full in less than an hour of hunting.

We told Kenton we were going fishing the next day. I remember he had a red fire wagon car that had pedals under the front hood. It was the only one I saw on the island at this time. He would pedal it while sitting in the seat and we would sometimes push him to make it go faster. Sometimes he would let us get a ride. Gilly would get one like it later and would let us ride in it.

Kenton and his family left for the States not long after we met him that night. I and all the other children envied him and all the others who were going away to live in The States. This was always the dream of every child and most adults of Utila. It was during this time we would begin to see several families begin to move and live in the States.

We took our two cans of soldias and put them under our house floor with a big rock or a piece of wood to cover the cans to prevent the soldias from escaping in the middle of the night. Life for them was now over and they would be killed tomorrow and be used by us to catch fish that we would in turn kill and eat. Sometimes we would roast the soldiers and eat them, but they had very little "meat" so we did not do that too often.

We put our sack containing our fishing lines, hooks, knives and other things we would need on our fishing trip, next to the two cans of soldiers or "soldias". We also had another sack, which contained our fruits and water. We would fill a couple of plastic bottles with drinking water right before we left. We also had an empty five-gallon plastic pail.

It was now about 7 p.m., and we headed out by the Corner. In two more hours the electricity would go off, and everyone would have to fend for his or herself trying to get home in the dark. Everybody, young and old, gathered at least one night of the week down by the Corner, at the center of town.

We stopped by Mr. Tonce Bush's house by the lamp pole. He lived on one side of the Corner and

Mr. Edwin Jackson (later Mr. Emerson) owned a shop on the other side of the street. On the lower side of the Corner was a park for children, and next to the park lived Mr. Edwin and his wife Ms. "LuLu" Jackson. Their children were Jackie, Baldwin, and Woody.

Next to Mr. Tonce lived Mr. Peter and Ms. "Aetna" Morgan whose children were Lillian, Fredo and an older son. I saw Betina and her sister Esperanza. They were daughters of Ms. Carrie (Hinds) whose other children were Van Wick, Jimmy, Sammy, Carlota and Inez. Across from the children's park was a big two-story old-time house belonging to Mr. Alfred Morgan and his wife Ms. Chrissie. Mr. Frankie Jackson's little restaurant was also on the other side of the park.

On the bottom part of the big house was a restaurant ran by Ms. Beatrice White. Her children were Jackie, Dottie, Liz, "Lilly White" Georgia, and Tony.

The three of us went into Mr. Frankie (Jackson) restaurant, which was small. But it was surprising how many people, especially children, could fit in his place especially on a Friday or Saturday night. Mr. Frankie, with the help of his daughter Menga (Wienelle), kept everything moving at a brisk pace. His wife was Ms. Vera (McCoy) and they also had a son named Larabee.

Mr. Frankie's brothers were Purdy and Gainel Jackson. Ms. Vera's brothers and sisters were Fredo, Coolidge, Tim, Ben and Jimmy McCoy.

Behind the counter, Mr. Frankie was busy serving people outside from his window and also to the people inside the restaurant, which was no more than five by five-feet. It was unpainted and uncased on the inside and was always a favorite place for the children to spend their five or ten cents. Mr. Frankie was busy shaving ice and serving "con yucas."

His menu was short and basic: Five cents dry klems (Klim) which was shaved ice with Klim (powdered milk) and his home made fruit syrup poured on top. Con yucas cost 5 cents. Holly Hoolies for one cent each.

He gave you a lot of soft boiled cassava

(yuca), a meat of the day (chicken, chicharones, fried pork, you name it) all covered by the gravy from the meat and then his mixture of cut cabbage, onions, salt, pepper, vinegar and black pepper on top. Mr. Frankie was a brown skinned man and thin. He lived by the rocky road by Mr. Joseph and Ms. Lilly Gay Ramon's house.

Mr. Frankie worked hard and was always wearing a cap. His face was drawn out and sagging from the wear and tear of life. In the daytime, before he opened the little restaurant, he would roll his wheelbarrow around town selling shaved ice. You could buy a one or two-cent snowball (no syrup) up to a five-cent dry "klem." Every penny was important in those days and he worked really hard for his cents.

His wheelbarrow was designed and built specifically for selling ice. He had round compartments on both sides of the wheelbarrow that carried individual holes for his many different bottles of syrup, and in the middle was a space to hold his block of ice.

He would make syrup from mangoes, pineapple,

sour sops, crabboos, you name the fruit and he had the syrup. He would come down Sandy Bay rolling his wheelbarrow to the schoolhouse to sell ice to the children during "recreo" (recess). His face had wrinkles and he was missing a few teeth.

You could also buy holly hollies for one cent each. They were made of sugar and were hard and white. They became chewy after a few minutes of chewing. His little restaurant was an institution and sooner or later everyone went there to buy something.

I squeezed in the restaurant just enough to place my order. I told him I wanted a "con yuca". It was busy and everyone around me was talking. You could eat inside or outside where he had two small benches. I saw Ricky and his brother Eddie Arnold Borden and "Bullitt" Whitefield out in front.

I saw "Tony Man" (Reinaldo) Zelaya. He stood in the back, outside by the window, eating his "con yuca". "Tony Man" was named after his father Mr. Reinaldo Zelaya. His mother was Ms. Marelli (née:

Laurie). His brothers and sisters were Annie (Lita), Ralph, Fulmer, Maris, Sherry and Fern.

The back window of the restaurant lifted up and down to open or close, while the side windows opened horizontally. Tony Man was talking to someone about a fish he had caught earlier in the day, a barracuda. He said they ate it not too long ago as all meat, especially fish had to be eaten fresh, due to lack of refrigerators. You could salt your fish but fresh was always better

Wardo and Gilly were out in front talking to Clyde and Morris Woods about our planned fishing trip. Mr. Frankie fixed my plate of con yuca and gave it to me with an outstretched hand and I gave him my five cents. He took the nickel from me and for a moment he just stopped and looked out the front door staring at no one or nothing in particular. I looked into his eyes and it was as if he was staring out into nowhere and saw nothing.

Even though I was too young to put into words at that moment, what I saw sadness in Mr. Frankie's face. His face said so much to me that night. I looked at him and looked outside to see that his eyes were not focused on anything in particular.

He looked sad, angry, beaten and lonely. The look in his face said he did not want to be here tonight and he was sweating profusely. In that brief moment I stared into his face and felt for him. I hoped I would never feel the way he looked tonight.

I squeezed out of the restaurant and went in front to stand up and eat. I saw Charles-O (Charles Ramon) coming up from Sandy Bay along with his cousin Eddie Ramon. Charles-o lived in Sandy Bay with his parents Mr. James and Ms. Trilby Ramon. His brother was James (Lighty) and his sisters were Rosilia (Muffet) and Jennita.

I started eating my cassava (yuca) and ground meat with my fingers. I was hungry. Gilly and Wardo joined me and they started eating from my food. We talked about going fishing and went over our checklist of the things we needed for the next day. After eating, we moved across the street by the light pole where a few other young boys had gathered to play "helote" (hide and seek).

A few old men stood around talking about everything and everyone. I saw Mr. Theodore Castillo, Mr. Hanford Bodden, and Mr. Archie Henderson talking to Mr. Tonce, who stood on his porch leaning on his railings.

It seemed a storm was coming and it was going to hit Utila. Mr. Archie, who owned The Mary L, said he heard the news on his radio. He talked about putting his boat in the lower or upper lagoon for safety.

All the boys gathered around the light pole. There was Bruten (Henry Bruten Bernard), Roque (Cardenas), Wardo, Gilly, myself, Freddy (Gabourel), Hank (Castillo), and a few other boys.

The old men continued talking about the storm and it caught my attention. I loved storms. Living on this small island, we saw our share of Nor'easters and the children would come out to play in them. The men said it would be here soon and everyone should get ready. They said it could be a hurricane, which is the first time I heard that word.

Morris Woods was chosen to find everyone else and he closed his eyes to start counting. Everyone fanned out, running to find a hiding place.

We ran barefoot into the darkness. Me, Wardo and Gilly stayed together. Some ran under Mr. Edwin Jackson's house, some ran out towards Holland and some of the boys ran out by the dock. My sister Lola, a tomboy, was also playing with us.

We played for a while and then went to my house and again checked our fishing supplies. Everything was still in place and we said goodnight to each other. Wardo went home through the back road, by the marmey tree, and Gilly just had to go next door. Tomorrow would be fun.

I went up our steps and into the house to get ready for bed. The lights would be going off soon as it would be 9:00 p.m. in a few minutes. I took a glass of water from the barrel and washed off my feet and dried them with an old piece of cloth. We went barefoot all day and that made our feet dusty and dirty by night. I hugged my father and mother then went to bed.

Our lights blinked and that meant we had 10 minutes before the electricity was shut off. We had to make sure we knew where to find the flashlights, lamps and lanterns. As usual we lit the kerosene lamp and turned it down low.

The night was hot but bearable. I went to sleep fast and slept sound. Like clockwork Ms. Lydia's rooster again crowed to wake me up. My mother once again began the day by taking the slop bucket down to be emptied in the swamp.

I got up from bed, ate breakfast, which was fried green plantains, bread, coffee and a piece of meat. I went under the house and as if it was planned, Gilly and Wardo showed up at the same time. We took our sacks and headed off to Sandy Bay to meet our cousins Lee Lee (Leonard) and Tony Boy (Alfred).

We headed over the Hill and passed Mr. Felix Cardenas' house, which was very close to the edge of the hill and always had a great view of the harbor. He and his wife Ms. Edin lived there with their children Monterey, Roque, Carlos, "Majie" and Joe DiMaggio. Mr."Felix" once made me a baseball bat from the limbs of a tree and all by hand. I bought one from him for 3 Lempiras ($1.50). That was a lot of money but my mother and father always had "extra" money when my father was out to sea.

On the other side of the street was Ms. Sula May's house. She lived there with her husband Mr. Henry Bush and their children: Crawford, and later Whitney, Neil, Henry, Sherry. They used to show slides under their house and charge about three cents to get in. They were mostly cartoons, or as we called all cartoons "mickey mouse". Whenever my parents could afford it I went to their show.

It was early in the morning, about 7:00 and the sun was already hot. From this part of the hill, the view was always spectacular. I could see pelicans diving into the water down Sandy Bay and I saw the Mary L owned by Mr. Archie Henderson docked to his wharf behind his house. I also saw a couple of paddling dories being paddled up to the Point, probably to fish. The sea was calm but now a soft wind began to blow.

We said hi to Joe DiMaggio who was standing in the doorway of their house looking out to the sea. Mr. Felix was sitting on the top step.

We continued walking and came to Marmey Lane then turned left. We passed Ms. Annie Laurie's two-story house. She taught us all in public school and gave injections to people of the island, as we had no doctors or nurses. I would have to go to her house almost every Saturday before swimming to get an injection. Ms. Annie Laurie's children were: Max, Don, Merely, and Zina Lou.

We turned right at The Cabildo, the government office, a two-story building. We began to walk faster and we passed the public school on the left. It was a one-story wood building by the beach and the paint had worn off. It had an outhouse over the water. It felt good to pass the school knowing we were on vacation.

Right after that we passed the Methodist Church

that my family attended, except for my father who did not go to church that often. A plaque on the front of the church said it was moved to this spot in 1897. I thought of how long ago that must have been. As children we had to go to church, no questions asked. You either went on Saturday to the Adventist, or Sundays to The Church of God, The Baptist or The Methodist church and many times the children went both to church services and Sunday school.

Pretty soon we were passing Ms. Mary Jane's (Bush) house. I always got scared when I passed her house. She lived there with her children Alan, Fodester, Hoyt, Brenson, Erlinda, Mercille/Mercy, Lenaire, and Horace. I saw her talking to her sister Ms. "Gigi" (Bertha) whose children were Ruby, Jorge (George), Naida, Alma (Ligia) and later Aretha.

Ms. Mary Jane's brothers and sisters were: Shirley Crombie, Angela Hernandez, MacDonald, Lois, Bertha and Fannie Inez. Their mother was Ms. Ruby.

Most children and adults on the island were

afraid of Ms. Mary Jane's son Horace. He was the roughest, toughest, meanest, and scariest kid you could meet. You did not want to make him mad at you. And he was never shy in letting you know how tough he was. He would fight in a split second and you never wanted to be the one he was fighting. He was red like a hornet, but scarier.

As we passed in front of the house I held my breath. I looked to see if Horace was in sight and said a silent prayer "Please God don't let Horace be home". Suddenly, he jumped from behind a breadfruit tree in their yard. He ran out to the street where we were walking. My heart stopped for a second.

"Where you "rump rims" going today"? Horace asked us. Wardo, who was also crazy, said "Fishin". Horace looked at our bucket of "soldias" and our sacks. "I'll take the biggest "soldias" and you could have the rest," he said to us. "Nah" Wardo replied. "Let "im" take some" I said. "Ah could take everything if I wanted to" Horace said in a loud rough voice.

At this time Ms. Mary Jane called out to Horace

to finish a chore he was doing for her. He took a few of our "soldias" and went under his house floor. I was never more relieved to see Ms. Mary Jane. "Hi Ms. Mary Jane" I called out. "Hi son" she answered.

We then passed Mr. Howard and Ms. Vida Bodden's house. They lived there with their children Renegale, Ida Bell, George, Ann, Marie, Ralston, Eva, Willis and Esther. Mr. Howard was a skilled carpenter and he built boats, all by hand. There were no electrical tools on the island at this time. He also built headstones on the graveyard.

The family had a small sugar cane patch growing right next to their house and you could buy five-cent pieces. I bought one piece, which was about three to four feet long.

My mother would always make sure I had at least five cents when I left the house. Today she gave me ten cents. I had the cane cut in three pieces and shared with Gilly and Wardo. We bit off the hard skin of the cane strip by strip, then took small bites and continued walking. The juice from the cane splashed around in my mouth with each chew and it was softer than most on the island.

We passed Ms. Jeannie Bodden's two-story house. She was an old lady and she lived there with her daughters, Warney and Manda. She also had a son named Mr. Everett, who was Mannie (Elridge) Coburn's father.

Ms. Jeannie, along with Ms. Cancie" (Candelabra) and Ms. Phyla, were women who taught school in English to the children. We used small books called Royal Readers, which were printed abroad.

If your family could afford it, you were sent to one of these ladies to learn English. You went in the afternoon, after attending mandatory public education, which was taught in Spanish. I attended Ms. Jeannie and Ms. Cancie's schools.

Soon we passed Mr. Charlie and Ms. Lydia Munoz' house. It was built low to the ground on short cement posts and they lived there with their children Lizzie, Margaret (Tuta), Linda, Arturo, Carleen, Wilson, Danny and Cleary. I saw Cleary and Arturo in the back of their house by the beach, working with a fishing line. It was a big line meant for big fish.

Mr. Charlie Munoz was talking to his brother Mr. Shaylock Munoz who lived next door. They were talking about fixing a dory that had sprung a leak. They also talked about a storm that was coming this way. I wondered if it was the same one I heard Mr. Archie Henderson talk about the other night by Mr. Tonce's house.

Mr. Shaylock said something about it turning into a hurricane. He and his wife Ms. Patricia lived next door to Mr. Charlie Munoz with their children Densen, Larrison, Douglas, Erna, Diana and "Cherino". Their house was set on high posts. We said hello to Larrison and turned right towards aunt Mary Ann's house. They all lived on the beach side of the road. Mr. Shaylock had a shallow well in the cliff rocks in front of their house.

Me, Gilly and Wardo went down the road leading to Lee Lee's house. We got to the front steps and called out for them. Aunt Mary Ann was cooking cow feet and you could smell it from outside.

She would cook them with boiled yuca, bananas and chatas. There were a lot of mosquitoes in their yard that day.

"Leh go" we called out as Lee Lee and Tony boy came to the front of the house. "Ready" Tony Boy said. I saw uncle Edward in the back yard using a machete to cut off a couple hands of green bananas from one of the many trees he grew on his land. We said hello. "You boys going' fishing today I heard" uncle Edward said to us. "Yes sir" we answered him.

The five of us walked out to the main road and headed further down to Mr. Bud Bud's (Steven Ebanks) house. He was my uncle Edward's brother. They were sons of Mr. Asha and Ms. Julia (Ramon) Ebanks. Their other children were Alda Rose, Dorothy, Lem, Osten and Beverly.

It was a beautiful day and the sun was growing hotter by the minute. We walked further down Sandy Bay and in the road that had grass to the sides. You could find many frogs in this part when it rained, especially at night. As we walked with the sea to our left I saw pelicans diving after sprats about 50 feet out in the water. That was a good sign, because wherever there were small fish, larger fish would find them and we in turn wanted catch the larger fish.

We arrived at Mr. Bud Bud and Ms. "Ayeah" Ebanks house. Their son Steven, we also called him Stevo, was standing by the railing on the front porch. "We could go fish in back right?" Lee Lee, his cousin, asked Stevo. "Yeah" he answered walking down the steps to where we were standing. We began to get the fishing lines ready to fish. We emptied a few "soldias" from the can on the ground. Some tried to crawl away but they are slow and all you had to do was touch their shell and they would stop.

We needed a medium sized rock to smash the "soldier's" shell and use the lower half of its body for bait. You would tear the animal in half at the point where the pouch met the upper body of the animal. You would then hook the "pouch" of the "soldias" body to your line.

Mr. Bud Bud's house was built in shallow beach water and he had a low fence all around the sides.   It was built with buttonwood posts, which were pounded deep into the sea bottom and held together by lumber running horizontally on each side on the top and in the middle. We would have to walk carefully on the very narrow fence. With a small rock for a sinker you could throw your line out about fifteen to twenty feet out, which was good for catching grunts.

I saw a pelicans about forty feet out splashing into the water. White seagulls flew nearby. The pelicans took turns diving in after fish and today it seemed like there were many fish.   It was a great sight to see them hunt for their food. They would slowly fly around in a small circle looking down at the sea. When they saw a fish they would then stretch out their wings and dive into the water. At the last moment they would adjust their wings and come to a controlled splash.

Usually they caught the fish they saw from the air and most times they caught more than one. We took out our fishing lines (tied around plastic bottles) and each one of us took a couple extra hooks, some "soldias" and a couple rocks. We would crush their upper body and throw it in the ocean for scent after using the "pouch" for bait on our hooks.

We carefully walked on Mr. Bud Bud's fence to the back of the house to face the open harbor. It was a beautiful sight. I could see the lighthouse out to my left, which was built on the Point by the reef. A steaming dory made its way down heading west to my right. We left enough space between each other and threw out our lines. Seconds later I heard Lee Lee yell and I knew he caught one. He hooked a good-sized grunt.

The fish tried in vain to escape but that was not to be. It was about eight to ten inches long. Pretty soon we were all pulling in our own fish. Each time we caught one we killed it with a smash from a rock to the head on the buttonwood fence or a knife that cut its "throat". We did this as soon as we could because we did not want the fish to flop around and escape back into the water. We filled the pail we brought with salt water to keep the fish fresh.

If you left it out in the hot sun, the fish would quickly become stiff and would quickly spoil. We learned early on as children that dead fish in the hot sun meant bad things, and in minutes. Some of us liked to clean our fish as soon as it was caught and then keep put it into the bucket of salt water.

We caught many grunts that day. Lee Lee caught the most with about eight. The rest of us caught our share. We weren't there too long before we came back around to the front of Mr. Bud Bud's house. We took our knives from the sack and started cleaning the fish. The scales were flying through the clear sunny air and would stick on our face but we just washed them off in the sea.

Afterwards we talked about going down by the slaughterhouse to fish some more and to look for some "conks" (conchs) on the reef. We got our equipment and our fish together and headed further down Sandy Bay.

Conchs, like all sea life, were plentiful during this time and you could see them all around on the reef. There were also a lot of "sea eggs" (sea urchins). Walking barefoot on the reef was relaxing but you had to be careful. We passed Mr. Leo and Ms. "Leena' (Bernice Evelina) Ramon's house and we stopped to buy some beef scraps.

Mr. Leo Ramon would buy or be given the leftover fat, with a little meat on it, from the cow that was killed at the slaughterhouse. He would then cut it up into smaller pieces, fry it out, then sell pieces of the fried meat along with a piece of fried banana, plantain or chata for five cents.

Mr. Leo and Ms. Leena lived by the beach and had an outhouse over the water. Their son Juan was just coming out of the house when Wardo asked him to let's go fishing. "I gotta help my pappa", he answered as he squinted his eyes from the glare of sun. It was hot.

I saw Eddie Ramon coming down the road. His parents were Mr. Britain and Ms. Nora Ramon and their other children were Julia (Lee Lee), Chancelee (Papi), Dorothy Lamour (Putney), Shirley, Marjorie, Frederick (Dugga), and

Victorene (Pudee).

There were "mangras (mangroves) in the shallow ocean (sea) to the left of us and coconut trees and bushes on our right. We walked and we talked. It was a subconscious feeling each one of us had, that these were special times. It would be many years later when we would be able to fully understand how really unique a life we had as children of Utila.

In looking back, it was always the freedom we had that made it so much fun. Here we were, seven to 9 year olds, 5 miles from home on a fishing trip at the other end of the island. Along the way one adult or the other would question if your parents knew where you were today or just keep an eye on you. The idea that everyone looked out for each other was a general way of life on Utila.

We broke the tip of the young conchs, with rocks, that we found and pulled the animal out. We put these into the pail with the fish. You could eat them raw but their meat was tough when it was not cooked. Their shells were hard and not easy to break.

We came to the slaughterhouse and decided to stop and fish from its cement floor. It had wooden posts and a thatched roof. It measured about 12 feet by 12 feet.

We each got a big rock to break the soldias and soon started throwing out our lines from the back of the slaughterhouse. We were facing out to the harbor. It was a clear day and you could easily see the outline of the mountains in La Ceiba, 18 miles away on the mainland. The harbor was calm.

A soft wind began to blow. In addition to the pelicans diving and splashing in the water, I saw a "steaming" dory glide on top of the water heading to the Point. Its propeller created a long white line of white bubbles and the waves from the dory would soon roll into the beach.

I looked around the slaughterhouse for a while and thought about the times I witnessed the killing of a cow in this spot. It was a ritual, a part of the many rites of passage for Utila young boys and girls to see a cow being killed just like it was to see the killing of a pig.

On the day a cow was to be killed, we would try to be there at the beginning of the event, from the time they went for the cow. We followed the owners and workers up to the grass piece (pasture) to rope the animal. The children would walk and run in front or behind the cow on the way down to the slaughterhouse. The men who held the rope tied around the cow's neck followed the cow. Like I did with pigs, I wondered if the cow knew it was going to be killed today?

People would wave along the way from under their house floors or on their steps. They knew there would be soon be fresh beef in the market very soon. Once we arrived at the slaughterhouse, the children would stand outside to watch the killing.

Sometimes the cow would hesitate and put up a fight when it was time for it to enter the slaughterhouse. But the men pulled and pushed until the cow was inside and tied to a post.

The bigger boys sometimes went inside but space was limited and few people as possible were allowed in during the killing. The "ax man" needed room to swing. The cow's neck would be tied to the post in a position that its head could not move freely.

The man, usually from Sandy Bay, would get ready to hit the cow in the forehead with the back of the axe with such force that it would immediately drop to the floor. He was making sure he had room to swing the ax when someone reminded him "One swing!" The man with the ax just looked around and smiled as if he was confident he would need just one swing of the ax.

Sandy Bay was known for its strong men. Most worked both the land and the sea. Mr. Georgie (they also called him Mamadoll) was one of the strongest, if not the strongest man from Sandy Bay and maybe all of Utila.

He was tall, dark and had muscles all over his body. We children would stop him in the street and ask him to lift us up in the air with just one or two of his fingers. He was always smiling and was always happy to lift the children up. I remember seeing Mr. Georgie paddling his dory almost everyday going down the harbor to pick coconuts then paddle back loaded with coconuts. He was really strong.

The part of the killing that we as children came to see was now near and we gathered in the road. We quieted down, as all the men got ready for their part of the killing. In what seemed like slow motion, the man brought the ax up over his right shoulder. His face was now serious. You could see the muscles in his arm bulge as he swung the ax down with such a powerful swing that when it connected to its skull, the cow dropped with a brutal thud to the cement floor. The children grimaced.

Like the killing of pigs, a man with a long sharp knife would bend over and slit the throat. The dark red blood spurted out all over the cement floor and flowed to the sides of the slaughterhouse and down the cement into the sea. Flies gathered and the dogs began to bark.

The cow would be hoisted, just like the pig, by their hind legs to the rafters above and the men would begin to remove the cowhide with their sharp knives.

The organs would then be removed and carefully put into a big pan or a five-gallon pail. The cow would then be cut in half, with a right and left side of the cow hanging from the rafters.

They would put the two halves into a dory and a man would paddle the meat up to the public market by the government dock. I remember the cow's meat would still be jumping when it arrived at the market about thirty minutes later as if it was still alive.

Some of the major cow owners at that time were Mr. Pat Flynn, Mr. George Gabourel, Mr. Peter Morgan, Mr. Ellis Morgan, Mr. Hanford Bodden and Ms. Annie Laurie.

After fishing from the slaughterhouse we decided to walk back up to town. Tide was low and the feeling was good as we walked on the reef barefoot. Each one of us scooped up water in our hands and wet our heads, to avoid heat strokes. That's what our parents told us to do. I picked up a couple more small conchs. I saw Gilly had a medium-sized one and Wardo picked up two. There were many around the reef today as usual. The colors of the wet conch shells with the sun hitting them in low tide produced a beautiful sight. The inside of the shells had pink, yellow, and off-white color combinations, which sparkled.

We heard a loud scream from Lee Lee. He stepped on a "sea egg" (sea urchin) and got a few "prickles" (thorns) broken off into the heel of his foot. We went to his aid and he limped in to the beach and leaned against a coconut tree. He lift his foot and we looked at his heel. You could see the dark ends of the broken off thorns sunk into the bottom of his foot. Everybody dreaded stepping on sea eggs. For this reason I hated walking in the grassy area of the sea and the reef.

"Pee pee on ma foot" Lee Lee said to us. It was believed that fresh urine would help in the healing of the wounds and also help later on with getting the "prickles" out of the foot. We boys gathered around Lee Lee and together we all urinated on his heel. He was done for the day. We decided that right about now was a good time to start heading home.

We got our fish, conchs and equipment together and headed up. Lee Lee was limping and had his hand on Tony Boy's shoulder for support. Aunt Mary Ann would now take care of him.

We passed Flora May Coburn who was standing by her house. She asked us for a fish and we gave her two. Flora Mae lived there with her parents Mr. Tommy (Thomas) and Ms. Millicent Coburn and their other children Roslyn, Valerian, Victor, Enna, Rita, Thomas (Boo Boo), Flora Mae, Maggie (Mommie), Dalia (BiBi) and Andrew (Budda).

Mr. Tommy Coburn parents were Mr. Victor and Ms. Roselind (McKenzie) Coburn whose other children were Oliver, Tommy, John, Olivia, Rodeann, Victorine, Ana Mae, Enid, Norah, Hennicot, Clemson, Trilby and they adopted their grandson Mannie (Eldridge) Coburn. He would be one of the first people to settle in New York from Utila and would later marry my cousin Elsa Lee McKenzie and they had two twin daughters Elsa and Nancy.

Me, Gilly and Wardo said bye to Lee Lee and Tony Boy as they headed off the main street to take the road to their house. We took our fish and conchs in the plastic pail and they took theirs as they headed home. Instead of going home the way we came over the Hill, we decided we would go straight up the main road.

We talked about going to Mr. Archie's picture show that night and wanted to pass his shop to see what movie was playing tonight. He would write the title and the name of the actors of the movie on his big blackboard, which he would stand on the porch of his shop for all to read. He wrote everything with white chalk.

After passing Mr. Charlie and Mr. Shaylock's Munoz house, we came to Ms. Jeannie Bodden's house. Her husband was Mr. Jacob Bodden. Ms. Jeannie lived in a big two-story house with her two daughters and two sons: Amanda, Vernie, Howard, and Everette who was Mannie (Elridge) Coburn's father.

We passed Ms. Della's house by the public school. She was the unofficial town photographer at a time when it was rare to own a camera. She would take pictures of us children on

Independence Day or on your birthday. All the pictures were in black and white. She would send the negatives to La Ceiba on the Mary L to be developed and Mr. Archie would bring them back.

Soon afterwards, we passed the park right next to the Cabildo, which served as a dance hall where our parents would go to dance when they were young. In the park was an old war cannon sitting on a base of cement and we stopped to climb on top of it. There was also a statue in the center of the park.

We finally got to Mr. Archie's shop and stopped to look at the blackboard. It read "Tarzan, The Ape Man" starring Johnny Weissmuller with a short write-up about the movie. Everyone on the island loved going to the Tarzan movies.

"Ya goin'?" Wardo asked Gilly and me. We both said yes and together, walked into Mr. Archie's shop, which was busy. I saw Ms. Marelli Zelaya and Annette Bernard standing at the counter with a few other people placing their orders. We had our fish and conchs with us. Mr. Archie and his wife Ms. Lucille Henderson, lived in a house behind their shop with their children Archie, Margaret, Annie Lou, Jeannette, Betty Joe, "Baba" (Barbara), and Effi Jane.

Gilly had two cents and bought 4 "black candies. They were small, round and black with white stripes running up and down the sides. He kept two and gave Wardo and me one each. These were very popular with the children because they were so cheap. If you had another two cents, you could buy some klem (Klim-powdered milk) to dip the black candy. We set off for home again with our fish and conchs.

I wanted to buy a bun sandwich from Mr. Archie but I did not have enough money. He sold the best bun sandwiches on the island. He charged 5 to 10 cents and they were great. On e fresh cut bun he would spread mayonnaise and mustard on the sides. Then they would add a slice or two of yellow cheese and a slice salami or sausage. The week before, the three of us shared one and a fresco (soda), which together cost ten cents. We sat out on the porch of Mr. Archie's shop with the sandwich. Gilly gave us a half to share and he took the other half.

We saw Mr. Milio (Emilio) and his bother Sweeney Castillo walking uptown with a stick shaped liked a bat. They said they were going to test it. Mr. Theodore Castillo had a house on the Point, and in the yard was a tree from which hung a long gas metal canister, which had washed ashore. It looked like a torpedo from a submarine and was about 5 to 7 feet long. They used it to announce the time, daylight hours, for the people of Utila.

The Castillo's would hit the hanging canister with a stick every hour on the hour from morning to sunset. One hit meant it was one o'clock. Two hits meant it was 2 o'clock and so on. You could hear it from almost anywhere on the island. Each hit by one of the Castillo boys would produce a loud "boom". The trick was to be sure you heard the first hit, or that could be the difference of it being ten o'clock or eleven.

We took our fish and conchs home to our houses for our parents to fry. My mother was happy that I had caught some fish and took them from me along with 2 or 3 small conchs. She went upstairs into the house to prepare them, at least put salt on them. Our grandmother, Gram, told Gilly he did a good job and also took his fish to go inside her house to begin supper. Wardo took his fish home and aunt Irene fried them for the family. We all had fried fish with fried green bananas that day.

While lying in bed that night, I thought about how happy I felt to go fishing during the day. We went many times like this fishing in the years ahead.

Chapter Three

Days turned into weeks and we played marbles, made slingshots and flew kites. We hunted for birds and iguanas and we played a lot of baseball.

It was Saturday, which meant it was time to "bathe" or swim in the sea. Me, and my sister Lola like most children, had specific chores we had to do on Saturdays before we were allowed to go swimming. We always started working on our chores right after eating breakfast.

We had to sweep out the house, oil the wood floors with distillate and sweep the yard. We would then burn the heaps of dried leaves. A couple hours after eating dinner (lunch), the children from all over the island would meet down by Mr. Archie's dock and right next to it was his daughter Ms. Jeannette and her husband Mr. Albert Zuniga's house by the beach to swim.

My mother gave me ten cents to buy some distillate from Mr. Archie's shop. I took a small plastic bottle and headed down the Hill.

Distillate is a liquid cousin of gasoline and kerosene. With a rag, we would wipe it into the flooring of the whole house, while crawling on our knees. They said it kept the "grubs" (termites) from eating the wood.

I walked past Ms. Julia and then Mr. Nulfo Ramos' house to the road. At the bottom of the Hill on the left next to Mr. Spurgeon's house lived Mr. "Alo" and Ms. Mayfern Pereira. Their children were: Billy Mays, Fannie, McAdoo, Aida, Meyers and they also had another son.

In the back of both houses lived Sally Ann, Mickey, Jack, John and Ruth. Their parents were Mr. Meyers and Ms. "Nollie" Pereira. I saw Mickey coming from his grand parents home and we said hi. I asked him about a big kite he and his brothers were building and he said they were finished and they would fly it later in the day. When I got to the Corner, I saw Mr. "Tata" walking slow and bent over, heading up to the Point where he lived. He had a little addition to his house (a "stanco") where he sold cheap white rum.

I turned to go down towards Sandy Bay. I arrived at Mr. Archie's shop and went inside and once again it was crowded with people two deep at the counter waiting to be served. I saw Ms. Hannah, Ms. Beatrice Bush, and Ms. Iris Hill among others calling out their list to Mr. Archie, Ms. Lucille and/or one of their daughters.

All you could hear was, "Gimmee" five cents of this or three cents of that or one pound of meat, flour or sugar from the women.

I saw my cousin Maxine (Pucci) come into the shop and she called out to me. She could help me get served faster as she worked for Mr. Archie. She was my cousin cousin. "Wha ya want" Maxine asked. "Ten cents distillate" I told her. She waived me to the middle of the shop through a gate and to the back. She asked someone to serve me.

Mr. Archie was rushing everyone, customers and workers alike and he was serving nonstop. I saw Bibi (Dalia) Ramon at the counter, calling out her list to Ms. Lucille. In the back was where

Mr. Archie kept his distillate, kerosene and gasoline in drums.

I got my ten cents worth of distillate and headed home. I saw "(Norman) Maburry" (Flynn) and asked him if he was going swimming and he said yes. Maburry lived on the Hill down by the Valley. His parents were Mr. Grover and Ms. Cecile Flynn. Their children were Judith, Dorothy, Tia, Tom, (Norman) Maburry and Roy.

A lot of children were doing chores before they went to "bathe in the sea". I saw Dewey (Zelaya) from the Point going down and said hi.

"How the mangoes?" he asked. "A lot." I said. "Ah goin' up tomorrow to pick up some". He said to me. Dewey lived on the Point with his parents Mr. "Rafile"/Rafael and Ms. Emma Zelaya. His brothers and sisters were Rafael/"Rafaelito", Reynolds, Nena and he had another brother.

His father was a close friend of my father and they worked together as merchant seamen. After passing Ms. Chloe's shop, I passed their ice factory where Mr. Clayton Bush was cutting and selling ice for the Morgan family. He would use a carpenter's saw and cut one long block of ice into smaller pieces, mostly five and ten cents pieces.

When you bought ice, you would take a piece of string or rope and he would tie it around the ice for easy carrying. The ice provided by the Morgan's was important as so few had a "fridge". Most people would go down for their ice just before noon. We would make lemonade, tamarind juice, Kool-Aid or juice drinks from any flavor of fruits that were in season.

I turned left at the corner and headed home. When I reached our yard my sister was yelling at me. She said I took the easy chore of going to the store while she had to sweep out the house. My sister and me were always fighting and arguing with each other.

We settled down and started to oil the floor. We began by soaking our rags with the distillate and wiping it on the floor until one area was covered then we would move to the next part of the house. When the whole floor was done we would move outside to rake up the leaves into heaps and then burn them. We loved to watch the fire and smoke made by the burning of the leaves.

On Saturdays you could see heaps of leaves burning all over the Hill. In the front of our house to the left of Mr. Alfred and Ms. Nessie Ponce lived Mr. Johnny Bodden and Ms. Emmaline (Mimi). Mr. Johnny was an old black man who played the violin, which he kept in a nice looking black case. I saw him on his porch playing music and I stopped to listen while my heap of dried leaves burned.

I said hi to Gram who was sweeping out her house. She looked old and she worked hard. She made the best "flittas" (fritters) that I ever tasted.

We finished our chores and took a rest before eating dinner (lunch). At the kitchen table we sat down and listened to the radio show "Chi Chi" from a station in Belize. Everyone who had a radio on the island would listen to the tales of this young girl. We listened quietly to the tales of Chi Chi while we quietly ate our food.

"Sista!" someone called out from in front of the

house. My sister went outside to meet Muggie (Gabourel) and Normita (Hinds). Janet Ponce was also outside by her house waiting on the girls. Muggie called out and my sister went to the front of the house and down the steps to talk with them. "Ah coming back", my sister said to me as she walked off barefoot with the girls. They walked down the Hill to Ms. Judith's house. I reminded my sister that we were going swimming soon. "Ah know", she answered.

Half an hour later she came back and we prepared to walk down to Ms. Annie Laurie's to get my weekly injection before we went swimming. Like many children on the island, my sister had her two dried coconuts (in their husks) with a rope tied securely to each one, which we used as life preservers. Dry coconuts will always float. I had my own dry coconut preserver as did many other children learning to swim.

We walked over the Hill to Sandy Bay where Ms. Annie Laurie lived. We passed Beryl Cooper in her front yard. The sun was clear and hot. I saw a beautiful red bird in a tree as we passed Mr.

Felix (Cardenas) house. This was not the bird-hunting season so today he flew freely. We would go during the rainy season, and summer, with slingshots in hand, hunting for birds in the bush. Every boy it seemed had a hand-made slingshot that they carved themselves.

We went from tree to tree to find that perfect small limb that had the Y shape. Sometimes it would take hours or days to finally cut the right limb.

All boys had a slingshot and hunted together from around six or seven years old, maybe earlier.

I looked at the bird fly away to my right. Soon we were at Ms. Annie Laurie's house. We went inside and she gave me the injection and we said goodbye to her and walked off to go uptown to swim. As we turned the corner we passed Mr. Pat Flynn's shop.

I saw his son Patrick and his daughter Hannah inside and asked Patrick what he was doing. He said he was straightening out the "bread-kind" (yuca, bananas, plantains, etc, which they sold in the shop). His father had a lot of land and cows.

We then passed Ms. Nina's house on the left. She had a well in her yard with a three to four feet cement wall around the top. Ms. Nina rarely came out of her house. We then passed the one-room kindergarten house where Ms. Annie Laurie taught kindergarten to almost everyone at one time or the other. I looked up to my left to see the hill we had just walked down up above. I now was looking up at Mr. Felix Cardenas' house.

On my right were homes that were built by the beach looking out into the harbor. We passed Kara Kay and Laverne Bush house where they lived with their brother Martin, and their parents Mr. Edwardo/Eduardo and Ms. Hettie Bush, who was later be killed by the propeller of a small plane on the airstrip up by the baseball field. Everyone who was old enough will always remember that day. We were in school when we heard the news and we all ran up to the field. Small one-propeller planes would come and landed on the baseball field or later on a strip up Jericho, where there was also a banana plantation. They had hundreds and hundreds of banana trees planted in neat long rows that looked so beautiful.

When we heard the sound of the plane's engine, we would all run up to the airfield to see who came and some boys would go to get a "chamba" or a job to carry down the person's suitcases. You could make ten or twenty five cents but you had to be strong. Most of us boys and girls ran up to the field to see a plane and to stand in back of it when it was preparing to start its run down the air strip for a takeoff.

We would stand in back of the plane to feel the wind it would propel at us. We did it for the fun. You did this with your eyes closed or you turned back on to the plane. We would run behind the plane after it started rolling away for a takeoff.

We would be making noise but you had to be careful, as the wind from the propeller would blow everything at us including much dust, dirt or rocks. We soon passed and said hello to Mr. Emerson Jackson who was sitting in his swing on the front porch. He lived there with his wife Ms. Ellen and their daughter Marie. "Good afternoon to you Marie." Mr. Emerson said to my mother. He was an old man and looked and talked like he was wise. His ancestry was English or Scottish. "Good afternoon Mr. Emerson." my mother replied. He would tell me many years later how plentiful the fish were when he was growing up.

He said sometimes when his mother wanted fish to fry, all he would have to do is take a "machett" (machete), walk two to three feet into the water and chop at the school of fish that would always be around the beach area. I looked at Mr. Emerson as we walked up and thought how old he must be judging from the oatmeal looking spots he had on his face.

You could now see the children begin to slowly move towards Mr. Archie's dock as we had a straight view of uptown. The beach by Mr. Albert and Ms. Jeanette Zuniga's house was now near and our Saturday ritual of "bathing in the sea" had begun.

I heard the yells, laughs, screams and

126

splashing of the children. We said hello to Mr. Reinaldo Zelaya passing his house on the left. I saw Charles-O and his brother Lighty (James) Ramon up ahead going out towards the sea. "Hey Buddo" Charles-O said to me looking back. "You ready?" he asked me with a big smile on his face. "Yeah" I answered, "I can't wait". I also saw Rano (Randy Scott) with a ripe mango in his hand heading uptown. My mother walked in the middle of my sister and me.

After passing Ms. Deccord's house we were now in sight of the children swimming. This was "the" place to swim for all the children. Mr. Albert and Ms. Jeannette lived there with their children Sidney, Archie, Kim, Janet, Connie Francis, Terry Lynn, Vienna Ione, and Geoffrey Vincent. There was always a large crowd of children swimming on Saturday afternoons.

Parents, all mothers, stood on the beach talking to each other while watching over the younger children. The older children were mostly jumping from Mr. Archie's dock where you had to be able to swim well as it was deep.

We finally got to the beach area and ran straight into the sea splashing water all over each other and laughing. We did not waste any time. "Be careful" my mother called out to my sister and me. The Caribbean Sea was warm again. But with so many children jumping and splashing you could not sea the bottom where we were swimming in the shallow. But a little further out, the water was very clear and you could see everything. I tried to stay away from the parts where there was grass growing at the bottom, too many things could go wrong if you took the wrong step. Mostly we were afraid of "sea eggs" (urchins). The sand at the bottom was swirling around.

I saw Tito Funez and his sister Julia. I saw Freddy Gabourel, Laura Cooper, Gilly, Wardo, Joe Joe (Joseph Angus Jr.) and Clinty. I had to stay in closer to where it was shallow until I learned to swim real good like the bigger boys.

I saw Morris Woods, Wanda James and Elden Bush. Then I saw Boozie (Clyde Woods) and his sister Addis. I also saw "Muggie" (Gabourel), Kara Kay and Laverne and Martin Bush. Almost every child was here today.

There were smiles and laughter all over the beach. Also swimming was Roque Cardenas, his brother Joe DiMaggio, and there was Hank (Castillo) and Dewey Zelaya. I saw Hoyt Bush and his brother Brenson and their other brothers Horace and Alan who were jumping from Mr. Archie's dock. (Paul) Alan Viera pushed someone from Mr. Archie's dock into the sea and was laughing out loud. There was a big splash as the person he pushed went under the water but came up a few seconds later.

On a Saturday, if you went out on the dock when the bigger children were swimming, you knew you were at risk of being pushed into the sea so you had to be careful.

For now, Gilly, myself, Wardo and my sister kept close to the beach with the other younger children. I saw others jumping from the dock showing off their swimming and diving skills, yelling as they jumped. They would go in "head fumas" (head first) or "foot fumas" (feet first) or the occasional belly stings when you landed on your stomach.

"Buddo c'mere", Wardo yelled to me about six feet away. Everyone was splashing, yelling or kicking water as I went over and he pointed to a spot in the water further down from where we were swimming. We saw a school of "fries" (small fish about two to three inches long and used as bait). The fries were cornered and jumping around on the top of the water. There were thousands and thousands of these fries swimming in what looked like a wide circle.

It seemed a school of jacks had surrounded the "fries" and were eating them. They made small splashes as they hit the water on re-entry after jumping out. Pretty soon two to three pelicans were diving in and getting their share of the fries. It was a beautiful sight to see. There were so many that sometimes you could see some fries jumping out of the pelican's mouth as it had caught so many. The pelicans floated on the top of the water with a pouch full of small fish, trying to make sure they all went to the stomach.

We then went back to swimming and swam for hours. Finally the salt water began to slow us down. Our eyes got red, our fingers turned to prunes and soon our swimming came to an end. We were satisfied. It was like this every week except during the rainy season, which lasted from around October to December or January.

My mother called out to my sister and me to let's go home. She also called for Gilly and Wardo. Our eyes were burning and we used to clap our hands together, bend our fingers to form a hole and look at the sun.

We passed Mr. Archie's shop and headed to the Corner to turn left. I saw Bullitt, from the Point, standing by light pole. He had just bought a candy from Mr. Edwin's shop (later Mr. Emerson's).

As soon as we reached home, my sister and I stood on the steps while my mother rinsed the salt off our bodies by using a plastic glass to scoop water out of the barrel and poured it over our heads. We then went inside and dried ourselves and changed into dry clothes.

As supper would not be for a while I told my mother I was going to Jack and Mickey Pereira's house to see them fly their big kite.

I ran slowly down the Hill and through Mr. Spurgeon's yard. When I got there I saw Mickey's sister Sally Ann standing on the steps of their house while the boys were gathered around a really big kite. It was about five to six feet tall. Mickey, his brother Jack and their sister Sally Ann were children of Mr. Meyers and Ms. "Nollie" Pereira.

It was the biggest kite I ever saw. Usually they were about one to three feet long and people used a thin fishing line or a thin string to fly kites but this one had a small rope and plenty of it.

They got it in the air and the kite rose higher and higher. The long cloth tail steadied it beautifully in the air. Younger boys like myself asked if they could fly it. Jack and Mickey said no but we could help by holding on to the rope. There were two to three or more people holding the rope. It was amazing to see this big kite soar into the air. In the back of the house was swamp and big birds, li8ke flamingos, flew in the front of us.

I did not wait until they pulled it down as I was hungry and walked back home to eat. I stopped in our yard for a while to play with Shaggy. My sister was on the porch playing with her dolly. I threw a small limb and said, "Go get it boy" and Shaggy did.

At dinner, my father confirmed to us he would be leaving very soon to Puerto Cortes on the boat to catch a ship. "You children listen to your mother while I'm gone, okay?" my father asked us. "Yes, sir" we both replied at the same time.

On the table were 2 small breads and my mother cut them into slices. We had butter and a piece of stewed beef. Each one had a cup of black coffee. My sister dunked her slice of bread in her cup of coffee like many people on the island loved to do.

"Dolores, don't forget to send the children their shoes," my mother said to my father. "I got the cut-outs you gave me," my father answered.   We had no shoe stores on the island. Our shoes were bought on the mainland, or from the States by our fathers who worked at sea.

To measure our foot size my mother would have us stand on a piece of paper and draw a line around our feet with a pencil and then cut along the line.   She would give the cut out paper to my father who would take it with him to measure and buy our shoes.

"Can we get a record player?" I asked my father.   "We'll see," he said.   "Don't forget to buy some Corn Flakes, canned peaches and fruit cocktail," my mother said to my father.   My father was always great in sending or bringing us whatever we asked for from the States.

"Dadad can I go on the ship with you" I asked my father.   "One of these days" he said with a smile.   My father would also send us books, comics, clothes, shoes, toys and various boxed or canned food each time his ship docked in Puerto Cortez.   Fruitcakes were favorites of almost everyone on the island.   His ships mostly took bananas from Honduras to different parts of the world. He would tell me stories about the many places he visited while working on the ships. He talked about docking at ports in places like New York, Mobile, Philadelphia, Italy, France and South America. It was exciting to hear him talking about his job and his life at sea. He went to so many places.

The children of merchant seamen were very fortunate as it gave us steady income in American dollars and we could live better and afford to buy more things than our parents when they were children. Those growing up during our time could now begin to seriously dream about going to the States.

There was poverty on the island but it was not whether you would eat or not, as the island supplied you with plenty. Between the land, sea and your neighbor, there was always enough food. It was a poverty of not being able to afford conveniences like a flush toilet, a refrigerator or other major appliance, or buy a piece of land. But now our fathers would begin to break the cycle of being poor.

We finished eating and started washing up. We got ready to go out on the town that night. The sun had set and night had come to the island once again. There was a full moon tonight and it was now shinning bright. My sister and me asked my mother if we could go out ahead and meet her and my father later by the corner. She said okay and advised us to be careful. She gave us each ten cents and off we went.

As we came to the foot of the Hill, I saw Aaron and CJ Woods (cousins) walking out to town talking to each other. "Wha ya goin' to buy?" I asked my sister. "Ah goin to Ms. May Woods for cake" she answered me. Yes, that sounded good. "Me too" I said to her. You could buy some of the best tasting baked goods on the island from Ms. May Woods' bakery.

At five cents a slice you could buy a piece of pumpkin, yuca, or chocolate cake. She also baked ripe banana and chata cakes and sold cookies. It was a small, unpainted shop located next to Edward's Dance Hall.

When we got to the Corner, it was buzzing with

children and adults. I saw Eddie Ramon and his sister Putney (Dorothy Lamour) and their cousin Elvis Ramon coming up from Sandy Bay. We said hi and continued walking up to Ms. May Woods's bakery. My sister and I got to the steps and went inside.

I saw Tonia and her sister Wanda (James) talking to Ms. May Woods's daughter Sheila and son Julio. They were laughing. My sister and I said hi to them and went to the counter to order.

Outside the front wood door, I saw CJ Woods and his brother Buggy (Murden) talking to Andrew Bernard and Aaron. They were laughing and Andrew's deep voice could be heard above the rest. They were laughing and joking about someone. Inside the restaurant was crowded.

Right away I saw a fresh baked chocolate cake and made my decision at that moment. My sister was going down the front of the counter looking at each cake trying to make up her mind. "Good evening" Ms. May Woods said to me. "A piece of chocolate cake" I said to her. She cut me a slice and I gave her my five cents.

I took a bite and my mouth watered with the taste. It was fresh, warm and sweet. This chocolate cake was perfect. My sister asked me for a piece and I let her take a bite. Chocolate was all over her face. She thought the same way I did and also bought a piece of chocolate cake.

I heard music coming from the nearby Silver Slipper, a dance hall. I had never been upstairs to see them dance. "Sista" and me saw our mother and we went with her to sit outside listening to the music and people making noise upstairs dancing.

We children danced barefoot to the music coming from the opened windows above. It was almost all country music. Then a song came on the record player or jukebox that we all knew and liked. We had heard it many times before tonight. It was The Twist, by Chubby Checker. There was a roar from the people upstairs in the dance hall and also outside by the children. We heard the first words, "Come on baby, let's do the Twist". We were making dust fly on the ground outside the second floor of the Silver Slipper. We were

Twisting and were having fun.

Every one of us were laughing, dancing and enjoying The Twist. While dancing, I said as a joke "let's go upstairs and dance". We were still laughing and twisting. Then someone answered "You can't go up "dare" (there)". I did not pay attention to the answer as I thought he meant we were children and were not allowed to go inside a dance hall.

But I decided to ask why I couldn't go upstairs and dance, as I was curious. "Because you're black," someone said. The words hit me hard. "Wha" you mean?" I asked as I stopped dancing. My sister then said, "He said black people can't dance in there". I froze for a moment and felt like I was hit a blow to my stomach. The answer flew around in my head unable to fully understand why. My stomach was sick.

I went to my mother and asked her if that was true. She said yes. "But why?" I asked her. "I will yell you…" she tried to say but someone called out to her and they started a conversation. The song was still playing upstairs but I did not pay attention from this point on.

I walked away staggering mentally. It had never dawned on me that this was the way things were, even though I did suspect something. Everybody on the island was good to each other I thought to myself and that was true because I saw it everyday. We went to church together, we went to school together and we always played great together but this was the only time I saw that the two groups, blacks and whites, did not do together. I did see some mixing in Edwards Hall where the black people danced. It was built low to the ground and the front door faced the street so we children always stopped to look inside. But the Silver Slipper was on the second floor two doors down so I never walked up the stairs.

I walked to the street in front of Mr. Rupert Eden's house where he lived with his wife Ms. Rosa and children: Bocita, Aubrey (Chutes), Doll and Curtis Dall.

I leaned against his fence trying to understand what I had just heard. I saw Davis and Dewey Buckley standing a few feet away and walked pass them. Their words were just blurs in the wind to my ears. My dog Shaggy followed me and I ended up at the end of Mr. Archie's dock under one of the greatest looking full moons that I could remember. It was spectacular.

It lit up the harbor and the island in a bright yellow light and was brighter than usual. It was so bright I saw shadows in the water of Shaggy, the dock and of myself.

So many thoughts were running through my mind trying to figure out reasons behind The Silver Slipper not allowing black people to dance with white people. Could it be that they were better than me? I asked myself. I did not believe that was true.

I thought so many thoughts in such a short time. Then for a moment I thought to myself "At least I'm better than…" and I ran through a list of children that I thought I was better than them, because my father worked at sea and was able and willing to give us almost whatever he could afford. Nobody wants to be the last, the worst, the weakest, etc. and tried to find a "scapegoat" of someone worst off than themselves.

Looking up at the full moon I heard something say to me that I was now thinking that I was better than others and I questioned that. Something said to me that what I was thinking was wrong. I then thought of how those people must have felt. I then reasoned that 99% of the islanders, whether black or white, were great people and got along real well.

Standing on the dock I kept looking up and it was like I was talking to the moon and it was talking to me. I was getting answers even though no words were exchanged.

I sat down on the end on Mr. Archie's dock with my feet hanging down. I rubbed Shaggy's head and he just sat by my side. I had learned something important tonight even though I could not fully understand. It was if the full moon had told me that not only was it wrong for someone to think they were better than me, is was also wrong for me to think that I was better than someone else. The full moon was always there for me and tonight we talked. Shaggy barked and the moon spoke.

My sister found me out on the dock and said my mother was calling me. We headed off, with Shaggy following, to meet my mother. I saw "aunt Becca" and her daughter Ms. Hannah standing in the street. Ms. Hannah's children were Angel, Walter, Efrain, Edgardo Carla, Rene, Hannah, Ina Lee, Tona and Juan (Juancito). I bought and shared a fresco (soda) with my sister and walked with her to the corner where my mother was waiting for us. I saw my father talking to the older men.

I walked home with my mother and my sister and we talked along the way. I would not bring up the subject of The Silver Slipper but I had learned a lot about life and myself that night even though it would be years for it to make complete sense.

I finally went to sleep that night and woke up to Shaggy barking and Ms. Lydia's rooster crowing. I went out to look and found he had killed a snake. I picked up the snake on a stick and showed it to my mother who threw Shaggy a bone from the leftovers the night before.

It was Sunday, which meant all the children had to go to Sunday school. This was a must for the great majority of the children. I started getting ready after breakfast by "washing up", brushing my teeth putting on my shoes and socks. This was the day of the week where you had to wear shoes if you had a pair otherwise you washed your feet and still went to Sunday school.

My sister Lola and I walked down the Hill to go to the Methodist and Church of God services as many children went to both churches. I saw many children, all in our finest, wearing shoes and walking to church.

It was a tradition to go walking behind the Point after Sunday school and we set off this afternoon. Today the wind began to slowly blow in, and you could see the waves slowly getting bigger. We passed the Baptist Church and then Mr. Harvey Morgan's house where he lived with his wife Ms. Zoila. They raised Julio Olin and "Jimbo".

In front of Mr. Harvey, lived Mr. "Tata". I also saw Mr. Durant, who was walking down from his house to town and he mentioned to Mr. Harvey that a hurricane was coming our way. Once again I paid attention to this word "hurricane".

Walking with my sister and me were Boozie, Gilly, Wardo and Morris Woods.

As we walked, we joked and we played games. Practically no shops were ever open on Sundays, or for that matter no other kind of business. It was a day of rest and the Sabbath was taken seriously on the island. The small number of islanders who did not abide by Saturday or Sunday being a holy day of rest and worship were very few. I saw Tito Funez ahead laughing and joking with some other boys on the side of the road.

We passed Laura Cooper's house where she lived with her brother Michael and sisters Margaret, Eileen and Mary. Their parents were Mr. Kester and his wife Ms. Irene Cooper. I saw Johnny Buckley sitting on the steps of the house he lived in with his parents Mr. John and Ms. Alda Buckley. Soon after we passed Mr. Pershing Howell's house on the right.

Mr. Pershing was a seaman, a boat builder, and

a farmer. He lived there with Ms. Ellen (Nee White). He had a large family including his niece Rose (Smith). We then passed Mr. Otis and Ms. Zola Feurtado's house. Their children were Frank, Wesby, Boyd, Dave and a sister named Eldean.

We came to the foot of the old wooden bridge and everyone took his or her time crossing over, as it was always an event. We stopped and looked over the edge to see the ocean (sea) below.

We tried to see the fish or "congor" eels below. We threw rocks into the water to see the splashes they would make. Depending on the tide, the water could go from clear to muddy. If the tide was flowing out from the lagoon, it was muddy and if it was flowing into the lagoon it was clear water.

I saw Larrison Munoz walking in front telling jokes that made everyone laugh. His father, Mr. Shaylock Munoz and his uncle, Mr. Charlie Munoz were among the best storytellers on the island and Larrison took right after the both of them. Today he was nothing but teeth with his laughter.

As we crossed the bridge, we followed a narrow

road that led to an open place where we would swim (in the white hole but not on Sundays) or look for fruits such as almonds and coco plums. There were many coconut trees on both the left and the right hand side of the road. There were no homes Blackbirds flew through the trees and pelicans dove in the water on the right. There was a line of children walking up the narrow road. This was your typical Sunday afternoon on Utila.

Reaching the "back of the Point", we played, ran around and through the bushes, ate fruits and threw rocks into the water. It was another beautiful day on the island. Everyone noticed the wind getting stronger as we began heading home.

Walking down I saw Ernie (Ernest) Hill standing on the porch of their family home. His parents were Mr. Simeon and Ms. Twyla Hill and his brothers and sister were Henry (Bucky), Billy, Johnny (Ringo) and Amy. Ernie asked me about the mangoes up our way and I told him there were a lot. Mr. Simeon's parents were Mr. Ernest and Ms.

Hazel Hill. Mr. Simeon's brothers and sisters were Natalie, Hazel, Henry, Clifton, "White Bush", Gwen, and Zola.

As we walked further down the road, we passed Mr. Fautee (Foster Cooper). He was standing on the left hand side of the street. He was married to Ms. Trudy (Whitefield). They had one son named Journegan. Mr. "Fautee" was talking to a couple other men about the storm.

Mr. Fautee owned boats, which ran freight. He also traded with companies in the U.S. that bought coconuts, bananas and other fruits. The Coopers were one of the largest families on the island along with the Whitefield's, the Munoz' and Ramon families.

Looking out to the sea on the left of us, I saw that the waves by the lighthouse were turning white as they hit the reef and splashed against the cement and metal base. Passing by was Nada Bush who lived up on The Point. Her parents were Mr. Karl and Ms. Vera Bush.

I said hello to Jackie Ramon who was standing in the street. His mother Ms. Beatrice White

(Ramon) had four other children: Dottie, Liz, Tony, and "Lilly White". I saw Jackie's grandfather Mr. David White coming up the road from town. Mr. David White was married to Ms. Dottie. They had Buddy (David), Beatrice, Estelle, Emily, Josephine and Aileen.

You could feel the temperature in the air change to cool as the sun disappeared behind the dark clouds. We soon passed Mr. Ellis Morgan's house as we walked down heading to the Corner. I saw Bradley (Brado) under his house floor. Their house was right by the beach and it was built on tall posts. Bradley's parents were Mr. Ellis and his wife Ms. Ula Morgan. His brothers and sisters were Ula Kay, Dottie, Russell, Gesner and Randy.

Passing their house I looked straight out to the ocean and again I noticed the waves splashing and rolling as far out as the eye could see.

We reached the Corner and there were a few people standing next to the light pole talking about the weather. The men said the storm was now a hurricane and would hit Utila in one to two days. I walked up Cola (de) Mico road with my sister. The tall mango trees in Mr. Spurgeon's yard were swaying back and forth. Normally you would get gusts or broken wind patterns but this wind was different, it was steady and just kept coming.

We got home and my mother was making supper. "There's a hurricane coming" my father called out from the bedroom. "Make sure we get extra batteries and kerosene," he said to my mother. On ordinary nights, flashlights and/or lanterns were a necessity but when storms came they were a must. You had to know where these items were every night of your life.

"Let's eat" my mother called out to us. We ate fast. We had coffee, home made bread and stewed chicken. My father had killed a chicken earlier in the day. I missed it this time but when it was time to kill a hen my father would let me be there to see. First we would run after the chicken if we had not decided to catch her as she left the coop in the morning. He would take the chicken in his left hand with its wings held behind it's back. He would then lay the hen's neck on a big root of a mango tree behind our house. Then he would quickly chop off its head with a quick swing of a "machett" (machete).

Witnessing this event several times, I would look into the chicken's eye as my father held the hen tight against the root. The chickens always made a lot of noise and jumped while being held. As I looked into its eye I wondered if the chicken knew that it was going to be killed. It was over in a second.

With its head cut off and on the ground, the body would be jumping and flapping in my fathers hand. The blood would gush from its neck. My father then gave the dead chicken to my mother who had a pot of hot water ready on the stove. She poured it on the chicken's body to loosen up its feathers then pulled them off by hand. She would then proceed to cut the chicken into pieces and then cook it, throwing the scraps to Shaggy.

We said our grace like we did before each and every meal. My father was feeling good ever since he got his call to catch a ship and begin a new stint of work at sea.

"Dadad please buy me a record player" I asked my father again. "Don't worry, you'll get it," he answered. "And some records" I said. My sister, "sista" (Lola) also asked for things like a dolly and clothes.

My parents always got us most of what we asked from them. They really spoiled us. Like most parents at this time my mother and father worked hard manual work and usually for little or no money when they were children.

I went out on the porch and felt the wind hit my body. You could hear the leaves and limbs swaying, swooshing and hitting each other. In Ms. Julia's yard the "cut-short" mangoes lay all over the ground. Our yard was the same.

We went to bed that night thinking about the hurricane coming our way. To me it was exciting. I loved the rain and the wind especially when both came at the same time. We never saw any great damage or any deaths caused by hurricanes, so as children we thought storms were fun. We had a lot of Nor'easters.

It was difficult to sleep. Mangoes falling from the trees would hit the roof with loud bangs and roll off the zinc roof to the ground. I listened closely to all the sounds caused by the wind.

We got up from bed early the next morning and started preparing for the hurricane. My parents were making sure we had enough fresh drinking water inside the house. We checked our flashlight and lanterns. We bought some bread, coffee and sugar. My mother already had breakfast ready when we sat down at the table. During breakfast it began to rain hard.

I stood on our porch looking around and next door I saw Harold James cutting some mango limbs from one of their trees that raked against their roof.

Soon it began to rain harder and the wind grew stronger to the point where we knew something really different was on the way. You could just feel it in the air. My mother gave me twenty-five cents to go to the shop and buy some extra kerosene, bread and coffee.

Many people from the Point, whose homes were directly exposed to the ocean, would make arrangements and stay with someone in their home on the Hill or Cola (de) Mico. Several times I remember people coming up to my grandparents, Joseph and Mannettie Angus' house when bad storms hit Utila and spend the night. The men would gather in one part of the house with a battery-operated radio playing, they drank hot black coffee. The women would be on the other side talking and would serve food to everyone.

I headed down The Hill to Mr. Archie's shop. In the streets were many children "bathing" in the rain. They were running and playing games, jumping and splashing in puddles. We children loved the rain. We were as close to nature as was possible at this time and place.

My sister Lola came running behind me and we walked together in the rain to the shop. In front of Ms. Leafy's house in the road I saw a couple of boys running and jumping in a big puddle of water. I saw Ralph Zelaya going up to the Point with his unbuttoned shirt flapping behind him in the wind. I saw "Alka Seltzer" (Rudy Parson) with Eddie Arnold and his brother Ricky Borden running around in front of Mr. Edwin's shop. Every one of us had big smiles on our faces and we were making noise, happy to be in the rain.

I held my quarter tight in my right hand and my plastic bottle for kerosene in my left hand. I stopped in the middle of the street, in front of Mr. Frankie's restaurant, and looked up and closed my eyes. I let the drops fall to my face and it felt great. I could feel each individual drop hit my skin and it was really coming down hard. As children we loved the rain and we loved the sun, it did not matter, all we did was adjust to each and had fun. We took what nature offered on any given day or season and ran with it. Today it was the rain, which would be followed by a storm.

During these summer storms the rain was warm. Looking up in front of Mr. Frankie shop I would blink my eyes every now and some drops would hit me directly in my eyes. I opened my mouth wide and felt the rain water go down. It tasted so fresh.

"C'mon" my sister called out to me. Heading down I saw Shirley Ramon going past us in a hurry. I got to Mr. Archie's shop and my sister said she wanted a black candy if there was any change left from the quarter. The trail of water from our bodies followed us to the counter.

Ms. Hermaine was at one end of the counter talking to someone. "One pound of flour" she said to Mr. Archie. She was a tall and "meaga" (skinny) woman and lived on the Point. There were many women at the counter waiting to be served with some men in the middle of the store buying batteries, flashlights, lanterns or lamps and lampshades, which were made of glass. I saw Mr. James and Mr. Joseph Ramon inspecting a couple of flashlights.

We had two cents change and we bought four black candies. I gave two to my sister and I took two. We each put them in our mouths and headed home. I saw Marion Cooper, running in front of Mr. Edwin's shop. Some kids were playing in the park at the corner. "Parque Infantil" (children's park)." I think they called it. It had slides and swings, and the ground was covered by beautiful white beach sand. The land belonged to Mr. Edwin Jackson and I believe Mr. Pershing Howell built the park. The kids loved it.

The wind had picked up even more and the waves were getting bigger and bigger out in the harbor. The ocean was beginning to look angry and each islander knew you had to respect the power of the wind and that of the sea.

The people who lived on the Utila Cays had already come up in their steaming dories. They were totally exposed to the storms with no protection from tress. All the paddling and steaming dories were being secured under people's house floors. The boats were already put into the upper and lower lagoons for shelter.

Going past Mr. D.D.'s house, I saw him yelling at Wardo. He was an old man who would yell at us if we played in his yard or with his hedges in front of his house. It seemed Wardo urinated by the corner post and Mr. D.D. was furious but

Wardo just kept running around not paying much attention to what the old man was saying. I saw Mr. Gideon Ponce walking fast coming down from the Point. He was the son of Mr. Leon and Ms. Lolita Ponce. They also had Miralda, Alfred, Leo, Victor, and George.

"Whey" you going'?" Wardo asked as he ran up to us. The drops of water were gushing down on us. "Home, then comin' back" I answered him. "Gimmee a piece of black candy" he asked, seeing it in my mouth. I took it out of my mouth and gave it to him and he took a bite. We shared everything with each other. My sister saw some other girls up ahead and went off with them.

I reached home and then hurried back down to play with the other children. It was Wardo, Elden, Gilly, Duke Snyder and myself running and jumping in the puddles and splashing the water on each other.

I saw Bradley Cooper and Ernie Hill. Every adult on the Point and Sandy Bay, especially those who built homes by the beach, were furiously preparing for the storm.

I saw Dewey Zelaya and Jackie Ramon running down the street. On The Point the sand had a silvery thick hard mix, close to the look of cement. It was a salty and sandy road. We headed up further and saw men pulling up their dories. You could hear them "One, two, three...pull!" as they dragged them under their house floors and tied them to the posts. "One, two, three pull!"

Some had a shed built by the beach in the water, where the dories would be hoisted up and secured to the posts of the shed. I could now sense, even as a child, that this storm was going to be worse than all the Nor'easters I had witnessed up to that point.

Many were working on batting up their windows. The sound of hammers hammering was coming from almost every house. Old wooden ladders were leaned up against almost every house.

I saw Mr. Sheldon Whitefield talking to Mr. Durant Bodden as they stood in the middle of the street. Mr. Durant's wife was Ms. Claire. We gathered around a puddle by Mr. Vernon and his wife Ms. Joyce Sanders' house. They lived there with their children Charles, Campanella, Victor, Verny Ann, Maureen and Ivelle.

The rain came down so hard and you could not see well. Everyone was now squinting. Out in the harbor, the waves were now made a roaring sound. They were coming one right after the other and the white tops collided with each other and made the ocean look mad. The water was now washing in further and further up on the beach.

It was now about 3:30 in the afternoon and the wind was making the rain come down with such force it stung your body when the drops hit you. I saw Campanela Sanders squinting but smiling as he ran past me.

Now all the adults were calling their children to come home. I headed down along with Morris Woods, Wardo and a couple other boys. We started running and turned the corner, heading up Cola (de) Mico road barefoot.

The tin on the roof of Ms. May Woods' house was lifting at the ends of her overhang. I said goodbye to the others and ran up the Hill to our `ouse.

My mother was waiting for me. "Hurry up and come in the house" she called as I walked up the steps. "We're going over to pappa's (grandfather Joseph) house tonight. "Why" I asked. We lived right next door to them so I couldn't understand why we would have to go over there for the night to feel safer when our house seemed strong enough. "That house is lower and stronger than ours" my mother replied and she said that this hurricane was going to be bad. I went inside my room, got a towel and dried up, leaving a trail of water from the front door. After putting on dry clothes I went to the porch. The rain was blowing in, even with our overhang.

I looked across to my grand-parents porch and saw men and their families from the Point were now coming to spend the night. I was getting wet again so I ran inside. "Let's eat" my father called out to my sister, who had just reached home.

After eating, we all ran next door. It was only about 30 feet away but we got wet again. My mother brought us dry clothes in a plastic bag and we went in gram's bedroom and changed again. Gram gave me a hug. From just inside the front door I looked outside.

With its long overhang, the wind still managed to blow the rain unto the porch of my grand parents home. The trees danced back and forth and threw mangoes, leaves and limbs to the ground. All the sounds were now blending together and made a unique "storm" sound. We heard the bang of the mangoes hitting the roof, the crack of limbs breaking off the trees and the wind hitting the leaves.

My father was talking to "Uncle" (Cleghorn Angus) and grand-father Joseph. They had a medium sized radio sitting on a table with the latest weather reports being broadcast from Belize and somewhere in the States. They changed radio stations every ten to fifteen minutes. There was a lot of static.

My father was telling the crowd that he took our horse Black Beauty and let him run free in the piece of land we owned by Pumpkin Hill Beach during the hurricane.

The children then went to a bedroom in the back where we talked and played games. Someone put a lantern in the room, in the parlor and in the kitchen. The public lights went off. Wardo, Gilly, sista, myself and a couple other children joked and then someone threw a pillow. Gram came in fast as she saw the pillow being thrown, and gave us all a good tongue lashing and let us know that she would not tolerate any more of this game. I stood in front of the radio and listened. The man talked about the hurricane. I listened to what he was saying but could not understand the words he was using. The radio used a large 4-inch square battery found in the back.

The announcer said he would be right back with more about the hurricane and said he was broadcasting from Dallas, Texas. I wondered where was Dallas. I walked over to where my father was standing and pulled on his pants. "Dadad" where is Dallas, Texas?" I asked him.

"Bud, that's in the States…" he answered. The sounds of the hurricane were everywhere. You could hear the roar from the sounds of the gigantic waves hitting against the "iron shore" about 2 to 3 miles away.

I heard our pig tied to a post under our house floor. She was squealing and making noise. My father and the rest of the men were still drinking hot black coffee. You could tell the coffee was hot by the way the sipping sounds made their way through the house, short and fast.

My mother and the rest of the women, who were on the other side of the house, were laughing and talking about cooking fish dishes. Mangoes from Gram's "Joe mango" tree fell like rocks overhead hitting the zinc roof. It was one loud bang right after the other. I can't remember all the people that were there that night but there were at least twelve adults and about 5 children.
The front doors were closed as rain was blowing in the house.

Grandfather Joseph was blind and sat in a chair by the table. He looked old, and you could see the many years of hard work and dealing with blindness all through his body. Hours passed and the only light in the house was coming from two lanterns and lamps. Almost every adult had a flashlight. Usually it was sticking out of the back pocket of the men who hunkered down around the radio.

The children found a place in the middle of the room and the women laid down on the other side of the house. The wind blew harder. As I lay there in my spot, I listened to the radio. There was a lot of snoring coming from those who had already gone to sleep. The excitement of the hurricane kept me awake. The man on the radio said something about playing some music for a while. The static disappeared from the radio and a woman began to sing. I turned my head towards the radio, as the voice and the music were hypnotizing. It was a beautiful song I thought to myself. Her voice was so clear coming all the way from Dallas, Texas.

The man later said the song was "Sweet Dreams" by Patsy Cline. Everyone on the island loved country music and I had heard this song before on my uncle's victrola. He would bring home country albums from the States. I remember him playing

music by Ernest Tubb, Eddy Arnold, and Hank
Williams. He would let one of the children
carefully wind up the victrola and then carefully
set the needle on the album and we would all sit
back and enjoy the music. The song, Sweet
Dreams, was the last thing I remembered that
night.

Morning came and everything was quiet. They
opened the doors and the sun came into the house.
Everyone went outside and I followed behind.
There were limbs, mangoes and leaves all over our
yard. I wandered off by myself. Ms. Julia's yard
was almost completely covered with mangoes. I
walked down the Hill in my short pants past Mr.
Spurgeon's house and again tree limbs and mangoes
were all over the street in front of his house.

I saw some sheets of zinc missing from homes.
I walked down to Sandy Bay and saw "Bunu" and his
brother Larry, sons of Ms. Rosalee. They were
coming down Marmey Lane Road where they lived at
the foot of the hill that led to the graveyard. I
wondered if they weren't afraid every night,
especially last night. Everyone on the island

believed in "duppies" (ghosts).

As I passed the schoolhouse, I saw it was missing a couple sheets of zinc, but still standing strong right next to the Methodist Church. But there was so much garbage over the beach. I saw many limbs, logs, cardboard, and plastic bottles that had washed ashore along with a lot of seaweed.

I saw Hoyt and his brother Horace sitting down talking to each other on their steps.

Again I was afraid of Horace. No matter how many times you passed Ms. Mary Jane's house, you were always aware that her son Horace lived in that house. I do not remember if they had a dog but if they did, I would be more afraid of Horace than the dog.

I prayed quietly as I passed but he never really bothered me. I saw Mr. Howard Bodden in fro of his house looking out to sea. He lived there with his wife Ms. Vida and their children Renegale, Ann, George, Ida Bell, Marie, Ralston, Eva, Willis and Esther.

I saw Lee Lee and Tony Boy (Ebanks) and we

walked down together. In front of Mr. Shaylock' Munoz house, the water had come up the beach and over the road to the other side. I saw Larrison and Elvis Ramon talking in the middle of the street. There were a lot of people walking all around inspecting the aftermath of the hurricane. I forgot that I didn't even tell my parents where I was going. The further down we went, the more debris you saw that the ocean had thrown up on the beach and across the road.

Not only was there lots of garbage all over, there were also many dead fish on the beach. I also saw many dead sea stars (star fish), sea eggs (sea urchins) and a couple of dead, sea horses, which were about six inches long and had died near each other.

The sun was beginning to break through and it became hotter. We were all barefoot and now wading through the water as it covered the street. Some men were standing around Mr. Britain and Ms. Nora Ramon's house. No one was hurt and the most damaged sustained was a couple sheets of zinc blown from the homes.

I saw Mr. Jasmer and Ms. Rachel Jackson. They lived in the back by my aunt Mary Ann and uncle Edward Ebanks house. I decided to turn around and said goodbye to Lee Lee and Tony Boy. I walked fast on the rain-drenched street, as I wanted to get home

The water must have come down by the buckets last night. Walking home I saw that almost everyone were now cleaning up. They had brooms, rakes and "machetts" (machetes) and that reminded me I had to get home soon as I would have to help clean up our yard.

As I passed Mr. Archie's shop, the sun really broke free and covered the island with a hazy hot heat. I thought to myself that the hurricane was exciting and I would always remember it.

Chapter Four

It was early 1963 and I was another year older. It was another hot day as usual and once again the morning sun came roaring over Utila like a lion. Sweat poured down your face and your body. It was only about 8:30. I heard there was a game of baseball behind Mr. Nado's house. We called the baseball field "Campo Nado". In the winter it was swampy and muddy but in the summer it was dry and we played baseball games there many times over the course of our years.

Someone said the game was moved to Mr. Marshalls' (Zelaya) yard so we headed off in that direction. We made noise as we walked up Cola (de) Mico Road. All of us boys were joking with each other. We were barefoot and the street was beginning to heat up.

Heading into Mr. Marshall's yard, I looked up Lozano Road, to my left, and saw what looked like clear smoke coming up from the street. They were vapors. I squinted and held my right hand over my eyes. It was really hot.

Ms. Hannah was coming down the road when she stopped to talk to my aunt Carmen (Cardona) Hinds. "What a hot day" Ms. Hannah said. She was right. Both women stood where Lozano Road met Cola (de) Mico Road. Aunt Carmen lived next to aunt Irene's house, in Savah, with her husband Mr. Elmer Hinds. Her children "Joe Joe" (Joseph Angus Jr.) and Fred Astor (Gregory) The Caribbean sun took no prisoners today. The sweat was rolling down my face like big pellets. This was nothing new on Utila.

The public well was not far away so we knew fresh water was near. We also had many fruit trees near so we did not care how hot it got today we were going to play baseball. In the group was Wardo, Mickey Pereira, Roque Cardenas, Clyde Woods, Elden Bush, Morris Woods, myself, and many other boys. Everyone was screaming, laughing, or joking. There was beautiful noise all around me. Baseball was big.

Those few who had baseball gloves shared with those who had none. The gloves we did have, were old, used and patched up. So were the baseballs and bats. We did not care. Some of the older boys were there including Hobart and Andrew Bernard, (Paul) Alan Viera, and Horace Bush. The older boys and men usually played up at the Concord baseball field. Almost every boy and man on Utila loved baseball.

We never threw any baseballs or bats away until they could not be used any longer. We repaired bats and balls. When the outer covering of the ball would tear off, we would sew it back on, and when the leather could not be sewn any more, we would wrap the inner remains of the ball in a sock and sew that up. When a bat broke we would nail it back together and/or put duck tape around it. Nothing was ever wasted.

Some boys brought hog plums, some brought mangoes and some brought water in plastic bottles. We soon settled into a competitive game of baseball. We were barefoot as usual and even though the skin on the bottom of your feet had grown hard protective layers, your feet still burned. I brought my dog Shaggy and a couple other boys also brought their dogs. The birds chirped from the trees on the other side of Mr. Marshall's yard.

Mr. Clifford Woods, a short and thin man who loved baseball, was standing in the road watching the game. He would yell out corrections every now and then. Baseball was played with passion on Utila and the men took it seriously. It was more than just a game to us boys. It was about friendship, competition, bonding, getting together, and having fun. We were free.

It was good that Mr. Marshall's yard was mostly covered by grass but there was no shade in the field. The sweat was rolling down everyone's faces and when mixed with the dirt from playing the game, it left streaks of dark lines on our faces and on our necks.

I was playing in the safe position of right field that day. It was closer to Mr. Marshall's front steps and left field was nearer to Lozano Road by Mr. Albert Gregory's house. As I looked in to home plate, I could see everything and everyone.

I saw Clyde and Walter (Alvarado) standing a

few feet from home plate, talking to each other. I saw and heard a couple of black birds sitting at the top of a tree chirping or squawking at each other. Each bird has a different sound and you learned how to tell the difference early on in your life. Soon there were about ten to fifteen blackbirds making noise. It was a beautiful day. Our dogs barked and played around with each other running all around the field

Wardo, who was one of the few our age willing to catch behind the plate, was waiting on deck. Being a catcher back then was tough. There were no shin guards, no cup, seldom a chest protector and then sometimes not even a mask. He caught barefoot behind the plate with whatever equipment he had or did not have. Needless to say he was hit many times by tipped baseballs.

The score was four to three Cola (de) Mico over the Point and we all gathered at home plate after the game. We had dirt all over our bodies. Every boy was happy.

We all joked around by home plate in the shade of a tree. We shared what we brought with each

174

other. Someone was passing around a plastic bottle of water and some passed around fruits. Each one of us took a swig and gave it to the next one down the line.

Mr. Marshall Zelaya was standing on the top step of his house and waved at us. We waved back and were thankful he shared his land with us. It was a Saturday, which meant that in a few minutes we would be going swimming or as we called it "bathing in the sea".

"Who's goin' swimin'?" Boozy (Clyde Woods) yelled out. "Me!!!!" everyone else answered at the same time, jumping up and down. Dirty faces were everywhere. "Yeah!!!!" we all screamed out at the top of our lungs.

The sun was beating down on us but we would soon have relief in the clear Caribbean Sea. Someone took the empty plastic bottles to the well and filled it up again with water.

The black birds were still "squawking" atop the trees, communicating with each other. There was only natural noises made and you could hear each one individually and clear. There was practically no man made noise. I looked around and listened to the dogs barking, the birds chirping, and the boys laughing. It was another beautiful day.

We all went home, knowing we would see each other soon and swim together down by the beach by Mr. Albert Zuniga and his wife Ms. Jeannette's house. There was nothing like playing baseball, getting real dirty and then going to "bathe in the sea". I got home and my mother reminded me we had to go to Ms. Annie Laurie's first to get my weekly injection. I really did not like getting injections.

We went over the Hill and down to Ms. Annie Laurie's house. My sister kept talking about buying a "penguino" (popsicle) from Mr. Archie's, when the Mary L came back from La Ceiba on Tuesday.

They would sell out minutes after the boat arrived and the green duffel bag containing the popsicles was unloaded. They cost cinquito (2 ½ cents) for one or 5 cents for a pack of two. My mother said she would give us five cents each on Tuesday to buy "penguinos". For us children, very few things was more exciting than waiting on Tuesdays down by the bay watching out to sea, waiting to see the Mary L pop the horizon with our "penguinos".

My sister and I went to the edge of the hill by Mr. Felix's Cardenas house. It was always a great view from here and I stopped every time I passed his house to look out into the harbor. We could see and hear children down on the dock jumping in the water and swimming. It was a really clear day and not one cloud was in the sky. It was sky-blue all around.

You could see many pelicans and seagulls flying and diving into the sea down Sandy Bay. Fish were jumping and when the sun hit their wet scales on their bodies, it produced a small silvery flash.

My sister and me talked about going to the States and how much fun that would be. We squinted as the sun beat down on the island. I pointed out to "sista" the gas vapors seeping up from the road and going up into the air.

"Ah bet dey ga (they have) a lot a cars in the

States." My sister said to me. "Dey got hundreds and hundreds." I said to her. My mother finally caught up with us and we continued walking down to Ms. Annie Laurie's.

We arrived and I got my injection then we headed uptown to go swimming. We passed Mr. Pat Flynn's house/shop on the corner in front of the "cabildo" (city hall). My mother was carrying our life preservers which consisted of two dried coconuts, still in their husks, tied to each other with a piece of rope. The dried up coconuts, in their husks, really floated well.

I saw Walter and Angel, Ms. Hannah's boys, walking up in front of us. It was such a ritual. Like clockwork, every Saturday afternoon we would gather down by Mr. Archie's dock and by Mr. Albert and Ms. Jeannette Zuniga's house and swim for hours. The smiles on our faces, the splashing and swimming, made Saturdays very special to the children.

We finally went home and washed the salt off our bodies from the barrel of fresh water, using a small pot or big plastic glass. My mother began to prepare supper and we all sat down to eat. My father announced that he would be leaving tomorrow, Sunday, night on the boat to Puerto Cortez to begin working again on the ships. We were happy and sad as we always missed him.

After supper we went to the bedroom and helped him pack his suitcase and we all talked. He told us to listen to our mother and to be good. Each one of us kept calling out the things we wanted him to bring us from the States.

We talked for a long time as a family and all went to bed late that night. My father drank coffee. He was happy to be shipping out again. He loved being independent. We all sat on the front porch and a full moon was out tonight. It was brilliant and bright.

The next day we went to Sunday school and then to church services like we did each Sunday. We ate an early supper and later went down to the dock to see my father off. We hugged him and he hugged us and we said goodbye. He got on the small boat with his suitcase and the boat slowly pulled away from the dock. I watched it disappear on the moonlight-covered sea. He would be arriving in Puerto Cortez in about eight to twelve hours.

We went home and sat down at the living room table under the dim light bulb. My sister and I decided to read some of our books. My mother always encouraged us to read and with my father traveling in and out of different states in the U.S., he brought us back many books. We had The Three Little Pigs, Little Red Ridding Hood, Jack and the Beanstalk, Cinderella, and hundreds more.

I really loved to read. The books made me wonder and they made me think. A couple weeks passed and Sunday night had rolled around again. It was a hot night and we were getting ready for bed when my mother came and sat down on the bed and called my sister and me to her side. She told us that tomorrow she was leaving for the States. It was a shock and I could not believe it. This would be the first of several times that both my mother and father left us alone with another family. My mother tried to comfort me but that was no help. She said my sister and I would be staying with Mr. Howard and Ms. Vida Bodden. I could not imagine my sister and me being alone.

My mother explained that this was the only way all of us would get to New York. She would have to go up first to work and save money, while my father also saved money while he worked at sea. I could not or would not understand that this was the only way we were to get to the States. I was the saddest child in the world that night. I wanted to go to the States but not that bad I thought to myself.

I went to sleep and when I woke up, my mother was gone and I was still in shock. Ms. Vida's daughter Ida Bell and someone else came to get us. They took us down to their house and introduced us and showed us the rooms we would be sleeping in while we stayed with them. My sister ran away that afternoon and went to gram's house. Ida Bell, George and myself went to bring her back. We all talked to her and after a while she decided to go back down Sandy Bay with us.

After a few days, the pain of missing my parents eased and we settled into a regular routine. They treated us well and we still had the same friends and went to the same school, as it was a small island. But I really missed my parents. I remember one, almost weekly, chore we had while living with the Bodden's. Mr. Howard would have my sister and me carry water in buckets up to the cemetery for him to mix cement to make headstones.

We would have to walk up the hill between Mr. Howard and Ms. Mary Jane's houses to the graveyard with our two half-filled buckets each. When we got there, we would bring our buckets of water to the grave where Mr. Howard and his other son Renegale would be mixing cement.

I would stand there and look at all the graves in the hot sun and tried to but I could not figure out death. It was always my understanding that only old people died except for one or two instances and I thought that we the children born during my time would live forever. Only one or two people died on the island each year so death was rare.

On the graveyard my sister and me would catch

small snakes and play with them. They were about 6 to 8 inches long and were round as a pencil. We would collect them and compete to see who caught the best looking ones. They were black and we would put them into our empty buckets or our shirt pockets as we headed back on our trips. My sister was never afraid to do anything the boys did and she loved snakes.

Since Mr. Howard worked with cement so much, the family would go down the shore in their steaming dory to get sacks of white beach sand and gravel, which would be added to the cement to make it strong. Mr. Howard was a master carpenter and he also built boats.

In setting off to get the gravel and white sand, Renegale would have control of the dory as he sat on the encased engine at the stern. He would have us push the dory away from the dock in front of their house. After a pull with his starting rope, the dory started and we were off. He would steam as close as possible to the shore as we headed down towards the beach past the lower lagoon.

This was the first time I was in a steaming dory but we would make this trip several times while me and my sister stayed with the family. We passed the slaughterhouse and the sound of the engine was loud and produced an echo. There were 3 rows of seats going across the dory and I sat by my sister in the middle row.

I looked around and saw lots of pelicans. They were plentiful. We hung our arms over the side of the dory and dragged our hands in the water. We smiled and we enjoyed our trip. You had to speak loud to be heard due to the sound of the engine.

As we approached the spot, a white hole, where we would get sand and gravel, Renegale slowed down the dory and pointed slowly towards the beach. We started jumping out before it got to shore. It was a great feeling as we hit the water and went under.

The sea was very clear even for Utila but it was also cooler than it was further up the shore. Practically no one came this far down the island. It was a white hole and you could see almost every grain of sand that was on the bottom. When you dove, without a mask, you could see even the little snakelike animals that had small holes in the sandy bottom.

Mr. Howard or George stood in the front of the dory and with a paddle, slowed it down and Renegale shut off the engine. They pulled its bow up on the beach and unloaded the empty sacks and shovels. They then started filling up the sacks, first one with white sand then one of gravels. My sister and me were left alone to swim with Ida Bell, and we did. We "splished", splashed, swam and dove.

I saw a couple sea horses moving slowly through the water. They were a soft red color and used its tail, which hung down, to paddle and move ahead. I kept diving and looking at all the sights at the bottom. I had no mask but none was really needed, as the water was crystal clear. There were many fish swimming around us.

About an hour passed and Mr. Howard called us in to eat as they were preparing to go back with the sacks. We ate the meat of young coconuts after drinking the water inside them. We brought along a machete. Renegale, George and Mr. Howard then loaded the bags of sand and gravel into the dory and each one of us got in. Renegale used the rope and pulled it with a strong jerk and we started on our way back up the shore.

On the return trip, the wind and waves were bigger and stronger than when we came down. The clear seawater splashed in our faces and we held on tight to the side of the dory.

Weeks passed and life went on. Then one day I saw Aaron Woods, (the mailman) walking towards us. My sister and me each got a letter from my mother. We looked at the letters and were excited. The envelope had red and blue stripes around the edges and it said VIA AIRMAIL. I read everything. Ms. Aetna Morgan used to run the post office, a small one room building located behind her house.

We opened our letters and began reading them. My mother would always begin with "Dearest Bud or Sister". She told us how much she loved and missed us. She wrote that she was working with a

186

family in New Jersey, in a place called Englewood Cliffs. In each letter was a ten-cent or a quarter wrapped in tissue or toilet paper. We would be so happy to get a dime. It was always so good to hear from my mother. She would send us letters on a regular basis and sometimes she would send us each a dollar, which was a lot of money for us children back then. One Christmas, my mother sent us each ten dollars.

We spent for weeks and it seemed we could not finish the ten dollars. We bought a lot of cake from Ms. Jeannie, Mr. Howard Bodden's mother, as she and her daughters baked delicious cakes to sell. We ate shaved ice from Mr. Frankie, and we went to the picture show almost every night. We bought cake at Ms. May Woods.

Months passed and we continued living with Ms. Vida and Mr. Howard and their family. One day I was playing with one of my small snakes in the middle of the street and looked uptown to my left and saw my father coming towards me. I could not believe it. I was happy and surprised. "Dadad!!" I yelled out. I dropped my snakes and ran towards him. My sister came running from under the house floor when she saw him. The three of us hugged each other. I did not want to let go. He was just as happy to see my sister and me, as we were to see him.

We would be going home with my father I kept thinking to myself. "We are going home" that is all I kept saying in my mind. He had come in unannounced on the boat and was going to take a vacation after about nine months away at sea. "Let's go home," my father said to us as he picked up his "valise" (suitcase). He said something to Ms. Vida and she said she would send our belongings up tomorrow.

The three of us walked uptown on the way to our house. Today my sister and me were the happiest children on Utila. We passed Ms. Mary Jane's house and for once I was not afraid of Horace. My father was with me. We walked, talked and laughed as we stopped at the dock for him to pick up two boxes he had brought for us from the States. "Killy" (Kilburn) and Lisha, two old men were carrying freight on their shoulders from the dock and were sweating.

My father asked my cousin Joe Joe (Joseph Angus) to help him as he picked up a box in his right hand by the rope tied around it. We were on our way up the road to our home and it was a great feeling.

My face was all smiles as was my sister's. We got home and opened all the doors and windows. After nine months away, I walked from room to room, enjoying the moment. I was home and I felt so free.

My father gave me money to go to the shop for some things we needed. That night we ate, we talked and we laughed. My father called us into the room and opened up the boxes he brought and it was like Christmas and your birthday rolled into one. He brought us Corn Flakes, a small record player with records, books, shoes, canned fruits, clothes and much more.

September turned into October and the rainy season was here again. My sister and I both had boots and raincoats that our father brought us. We were fortunate children. The time was nearing once again for him to leave and catch another ship.

One day in November, I was walking from Sandy Bay over the Hill. As I passed Mr. Jose Gomez house, I could hear a woman sobbing and crying as I drew closer.

I walked slower and saw that it was Ms. Lydia Bernard on her back porch. I stopped under a tree in her back yard next to our house. She put her hands in the air while she was sobbing. She was clearly upset. I stood there wondering what was wrong until I heard her shout out to no one in particular "They killed President Kennedy, they killed President Kennedy…. It was on the radio, they shot him, he's dead". A woman came out to console her. I think it was one of her daughters.

I did not know who she was talking about but I had heard that name before while listening to the old men on The Corner and on the radio. The way Ms. Lydia was crying made me think he was special. I saw the tears coming down her dark face one by one and they were big. "Calm down, calm down" someone said to her. She sat in a chair.

It felt so sad to see her crying. "He was a good man." She said through her tears. "They killed President Kennedy.", she sobbed again to another person in the house. I walked away still wondering who was this man, President Kennedy, that his dying made Ms. Lydia cry the way she did that day.

Chapter Five

It was a time when there were about1,200 islanders. Tonight just on the highway going, east there were more than in all of Utila during that time. Life was very simple as we were ignorant of so much. We just did not know much of what was happening away from Utila, but we were happy and we got along so well. All we had was "God and nature" he said that night down on the corner and he was right. The island lived with the belief of we would go to Heaven and nature supplied us with our food and fun.

We had the sun, which gave us an average of 85 degrees (F) or higher temperature most of the year. We had the crystal clear Caribbean Sea, which supplied us with food, fun and a living. We had the land producing the most beautiful variety of fruits, vegetables and home medicine. We, the children also had the freedom to enjoy what we had. We were free. With a small population there was room for everyone.

Memories of running with the cows come to mind.

I remembered how both children and adults would gather down at the center of town waiting for the boat with cows to arrive.

The boat would anchor about 50 feet out and the cows would be lowered by wench into the sea and directed to swim to the beach by a couple of young men who were in the water on both sides of the cows. They were the cow swimmers. I remembered this one of many times we ran with the cows.

The boat came in and the cows were lowered into the sea and were directed to swim into the beach. They would then be tied to one of the almonds trees in Ms. Chloe's land. I looked at the animals as they were put into the sea. Each one could swim right away. It seemed all animals, or most, are born with the ability from birth to be able to swim. I knew because we had thrown dogs and cats into the water and they would automatically swim. Horses could also swim.

When all the cows had been brought ashore, the preparations began with the young men who were guiding the cows would join the others to head to the bush.   Only the "bad" cows, mostly bulls, were tied to a rope.

On this bright hot sunny day we were now ready to break into a run.   The youngest led the way then followed by older children, finally came the adults and then the cows.   Screams of "cows coming... cows coming" roared out and we were on our way.   Sweat was rushing down our faces and our hearts began to beat faster with excitement.

For safety, we could run into Mr. Edwin's shop, which was low to the ground or we could run under Mr. Tonce's house floor, which was about four feet off the ground, or we would run under the house belonging to Mr. "D.D." and Ms. Leafy.

We had many outs along the way and we kept them in mind. You could also run up the Hill using the cement steps leading to Mr. Louie Mcfield's road. He lived there with his wife Ms. Violet and their children Reina, Stanford and Inda.

We were on our way running bare fee it up the road screaming with fun. "Cows coming...cows coming" could be heard in front and in back of me. I saw Ms. Patsy Munoz running behind me yelling at all the kids to get out of her way. A few children took refuge right away by running into Mr. Edwin's shop and a few ran straight under Mr. Tonce's house to watch in safety. Gilly, Wardo, Lola and myself kept running up the road. The idea was to run in front of the cows all the way to the "grass piece" (pasture). Few children my age ever made it all the way. We were just too young but our time would come when we made it all the way up.

More screams of fun and fright could be heard on the Corner, coming mostly from the children. The adrenaline was working overtime and this was no time to trip, stumble or fall. This time they brought a couple of bad bulls; some needed two ropes to guide them. Me, Gilly, Lola and Wardo said we would run together. I saw "Kimmy" (Kim) Zuniga yelling and running, followed by Tonia and Wanda James, Elden Bush and Maggie (Muggie) Gabourel.

I also saw Larrison Munoz, "Lighty" (James Ramon) and his brother Charles-o (Charles Ramon), Rano (Randy Scott) running behind us. I saw Sidio

(Sidney Zuniga), Murden Woods and I also saw Donald (Mr. Durant's son). It seemed everybody was there for the run. I saw Sally Ann Pereira, Dewey, Bullitt and a bunch of others running in one direction or the other, but most were just trying to stay ahead of the cows. We headed up Cola (de) Mico road running as fast as we could with everyone close behind us.

There were about fifteen cows. I saw Elden Bush and "Clevie", "Babe", and Barbara Bernard running to the side of me.

Many sounds, sights and smells came together to form the "running with the cows". Children yelling, dogs barking, the sounds of each cow hoof hitting the dusty unpaved road, the smell of sweat from the people and the animals, it was a potpourri of smell. My dog Shaggy joined Lola and me on our run when we reached Ms. Pansy and Mr. Spurgeon's house. We were now in a full-fledged run for survival, you could not slow down. Our eyes were wide and our mouths were opened wide.

Children and adults joined the run along the

way. There was Hobart and Augustus Bernard, Clyde and Morris Woods running along with "Maburry". Boozie was hollering and making a lot of noise, "Cows coming.... cows coming!!!" he yelled.

The younger children in front of us abandoned the run and sought shelter under a house floor or up someone's stairs. Now we would be the next to go as we were now in the lead with the older children right behind. The adults followed us. It was a fun and chaotic scene.

People stood on their top steps cheering on the participants. I heard someone yell from the back that a bull had run into Mr. Edwin's shop. A couple cows broke loose from the run and went into people's yards but were quickly reunited with the pack. Very few yards had fences so the cows had a lot of room to run free.

They got them back in line and when we passed Mr. Georgie and Ms. Judith's house, we only had seconds before we would be overrun.

My sister and me decided the crowd behind was getting too close and we broke from the run and dashed up Mr. Will and Ms. Norma Hind's front steps. We could not keep up any longer. Gilly followed us. Wardo kept on running, as he did not care about getting hurt. He had no fear.

From the steps, panting for breath, we saw the rest of the run. Some cows came into the yard and we screamed. They were snorting and mooing. The children and adults were screaming and the dogs were barking. Today there were a lot of cows and bulls that did not want to go along with the run as their owners had planned.

My dog Shaggy continued running with the cows and just a few more people brought up the rear and it was soon over. When we got older we would make it all the way but not today. Any and everyone who has participated in the running of the cows, remembers how unique an experience that was and will always remember it.

I thought of how tough our parent's lives were compared to ours. They worked so hard when they were growing up and at that time had few dreams and lived hand to mouth. Each generation before them had it even worse.

I thought of how my father told me that were it

not for World War 11 the island probably would have remained in the dark ages. He told me that during the war, the U.S. needed all its able-bodied men, and women, to fight or work directly or indirectly in the war effort. This produced a big need for foreign men to work on the American and foreign registered cargo ships as merchant seamen.

The need was so great that the shipping companies would send training ships and sign up the young men on the spot. You just had to be healthy and able to word hard. It was even easier for the island men because they already spoke English as a first language. They were strong and they were eager to get off the island, and they knew the sea.

This was to be the island's first big break and many took the opportunity, including my father. The men would now begin to earn real money, and more important the money would be in U.S. dollars.

Yes, we the children born on Utila during the 1950's and 1960's reaped the benefits of the improving economic condition created by the results of a tragedy.

There were many merchant seamen from the islands during this time. There were men like my father Dolores Cardona, Mr. Alfred Ponce, Mr. George Gabourel, Mr. Tony James, Mr. Albert Zuniga, Mr. Morris Woods, Mannie (Eldridge) Coburn and many more. They literally lifted Utila on their backs and carried us on the road to prosperity.

It was also around the early 1960's when the women from Utila also saw opportunities come their way. They could now get sleep-in or day jobs cleaning homes in the States. All you needed was an invitation letter from an American family and the money to buy your airline ticket. With more men now working at sea, women were able to afford a ticket. The doors were now opened wide on dreams of going to the States. Families now began to move north to New York and New Orleans. Utila would never be the same.

I thought of how some people during this time were larger than life when we were growing up.

Many people came to mind but one name stuck out from the others and it was that of Mr. Archie Henderson or "Captain Arch". It was not only how much he affected the children but also the adults. He touched everyone's lives directly or indirectly at some time in their lives.

He owned the Picture Show where we would go to see the movies and enjoy so many hours of make believe. We could see what things looked like outside our world even though the movies were from the 1940's and had just made its way to Utila. I don't know how he made money charging five and ten cents to get inside.

Our favorite movies were cowboy, war and Tarzan movies. Some of the favorite actors of the islanders were Johnny Weissmuller, Gene Autry, Roy Rogers and The Three Stooges who we referred to as The Three Fools.

Mr. Archie's influence over the islanders did not stop with the Picture Show. He also had a shop where most people went to buy at one time or the other. You could buy anything from bun sandwiches, "frescos", groceries, kerosene, gasoline and best of all, "penguinos" (popsicles) for the children on Tuesdays. Mr. Archie and his wife Ms. Lucille would always try to treat you fair. He was a man who was gruff and spoke his mind but he had a good heart.

Not only did Mr. Archie own the Picture Show and his shop, he also had The Mary L. It was a small boat, about 40 feet long but it was an important boat for the people of Utila. The Mary L was the most reliable link the islanders had to the mainland to the port of La Ceiba as passengers. It was only 18 miles away but the deep ocean in between could get ugly at times and the boats were so small, but the Mary L always made the trip except for the times of storms.

Like clockwork Captain Archie would leave every Monday morning before dawn, around 4:30 or 5:00 a.m. on the trip that took 3 to 3 ½ hours and spend the night in La Ceiba and return to Utila the next day in the early afternoon. Every child knew the schedule of the Mary L. One way or the other Mr. Archie or Captain Arch touched your life.

Years passed and my mother returned from New York and said she was now ready to take my two sisters and myself with her to New York. It was 1968 and it was one of the most exciting moments in our lives. My sister Lola and me along with our younger sister Linda were excited and happy. Linda was too young to understand, as she was only four years old and my sister Lola was 11. Mr. Rupert Eden came by our house and filled out all our paperwork as he did with so many families now leaving for the States.

It was at this time that I truly believed in my heart that the waiting was over and the whole family would finally be together in New York. My mother told us we would leave in a few days to be reunited with my father who was working and waiting for us in New York.

The morning had come when it was time to go and we woke up early to take the Mary L to La Ceiba. From there we would take a train to San Pedro Sula where we would then catch the plane heading to Miami and then another to New York.

There was a full moon and we walked down to the

dock and I looked up at the sky. I could see everything as if it was day but it was about 3:30 to 4:00 in the morning.

We made our way to the dock with my mother carrying our younger sister Linda in her arms. We were all excited. My parents had finally saved enough money to take us to the States. We really paid a high price, having to stay with other families several times and being away from our parents.

But now the wait was over and we'd be on the Mary L soon, taking the first leg of our trip. I looked out to the end of the short dock and saw that the full moon lit up the sky and reflected off the sea like a mirror. The sun would soon rise getting but right now the full moon held on. This would be the last sight I saw of Utila for years, a full moon over the harbor.

Mr. Archie gave commands to board the boat and everyone listened to him. There were four empty steel barrels tied around the base of the mast with a rope. He would be bringing back more gasoline and kerosene from La Ceiba to sell in his shop. There were a couple of large brown sacks (crocus sacks) filled with blue-back crabs from the swamp and you could smell them. Someone was taking them to La Ceiba to sell on the streets around the market for 2 to 3 cents for each. We stepped from the dock to The Mary L and walked down the sides looking for a place to sit down.

The boat had a couple of bunks behind the steering wheel, on the inside of the small cabin. These were uncomfortable to me and I always preferred to sit outside on the bench running alongside the boat.

Mr. Archie gave the orders and someone loosened the ropes. The deckhands pushed the boat away from the dock with their bare feet and Mr. Archie slowly turned the Mary L around and headed for La Ceiba.

We slowly made our way past the lighthouse and Mr. Archie started giving the engine more gas. My father would be waiting for us in New York, in our apartment in Harlem. My mother had to lie down on all her boat trips and would still get seasick. She got in the top bunk with my younger sister Linda.

The men in the back of the boat talked of everything from farming to the weather as they drank hot black coffee from the "galley". The small toilet was on the right. The morning sun faintly popped up through the ocean and the full moon would slowly give way to daylight. It was a beautiful sight. The time went fast as I looked out at the ocean from the stern of the Mary L. It was calm and we made good time.

After about three hours, land was in sight. Ahead was the dock and we made our way closer. The water changed colors and turned from a dark blue to a light green then a dark green color.

The sea then became dirtier the closer you got to the dock. I think the city's sewage entered the ocean close to the dock and the big ships stirred up the sand from the bottom. There was one ship tied to the large and tall dock loading bananas. The mountains in the back of the city were outlined and detailed on this clear summer morning. There were a lot of people scurrying around the wharf. Everything would now be in Spanish.

We docked in front of the ship. The dock was much taller, bigger, longer and stronger than our little docks in Utila. You had to get on top of the Mary L to get to the dock, which was higher than the boat.

A "plank" was laid across from The Mary L's top to the dock and everyone would have to slowly walk the few feet until they were secure on the dock. The "plank" was three to four feet wide and did not leave much room for error. It was scary walking across, because if you fell, you would fall right into that deep and muddy water.

The children and the women were given a hand by a deckhand on the top of the boat and another who was on the dock. My mother gathered us close to her side and we headed out to the foot of the dock to catch a taxi. Two men were carrying the two suitcases.

We got to the end of the dock and caught a taxi. Ninety nine percent of the taxis were Volkswagen Beatles that we called "cucarachas".

They resembled roaches. I loved riding in cars as we rarely got this chance, living on Utila. We got to the train station, bought our tickets and got on and sat in our seats. My mother made sure our suitcases were put on the train. We sat in one of the middle cars and the seats were made of yellow straw-like material.

The conductor blew the whistle and the locomotive started making noise as it "chugged" along trying to pull the ten to fifteen cars of passengers and freight behind it. The smoke rose from its stack. We slowly got momentum and were soon going fast on our way to San Pedro Sula.

My sisters and I laughed and played as we stuck our hands out the window, trying to grab laves from the short trees, which ran alongside the railroad tracks. We played with our younger sister and she was happy. When the train made wide turns we could see the locomotive up front pulling us.

The train made stops along the way and people would be waiting to sell to the passengers. They would have metal or plastic buckets and basins full of food and drinks. My mother bought us each something to eat and drink. We arrived in San Pedro a couple hours later and took a taxi to my aunt Elozia's house to rest for tomorrow's trip to New York. There were many cars and trucks honking all around us and I was not used to this noise.

Aunt Elozia had 2 daughters: Vicenta and Jane. Whenever we came to San Pedro we would play with Vicenta's son Jorge and he would show us around the neighborhood.

We went to bed and woke early the next morning to take a taxi to the airport. When we arrived, my mother, with Linda in her arms, went to the counter and gave some papers to the person at the counter. My sister and I looked out from the airport and saw a really big plane. It had four large propellers. My mother said that was the plane we would be taking to Miami and then another one just like it to New York. I never saw an airplane this size and stood there thinking that soon we would all be on it. It sat there in the hot Honduran sun.

My sister Lola and I kept staring out at the plane and talking about the fact we were finally going to New York. We were all smiles and then were advised that it was time to board and we walked out on the tarmac and started going up the metal steps that the men rolled up earlier to the plane.

It was hot and we made it up to the airplane's door and went to our seats with the help of my mother and a stewardess. My sister and I promised to share the window and I took my turn first.

We were all so happy and excited. I thought of New York and then I thought of Utila. I would be leaving all my friends behind but I would finally be going to the States to begin a whole new life. I sat in my seat wondering when I would be back and also thought about our father in New York waiting for us. I thought of swimming in the sea. Would I be able to do that in New York? The stewardesses closed the doors and the men out on the tarmac rolled away the metal steps from the plane.

The propellers went from turning slowly to turning fast in a few minutes. The plane slowly moved away and rolled to the end of the runway. I looked out at the two propellers on my side and they were now turning with great speed. The airplane began moving down the runaway. It went faster and faster until the trees on the sides of the airport became a blur.

I kept thinking about our trip when the plane started to lift off the ground. We were finally on our way to Miami and then New York. That frame froze in my head, the moment of me sitting in my seat and the plane taking off the ground. This was the beginning of an exciting journey and an end to a way of life, as we had known it.

I was born in paradise.

Thanks

I have to thank my parents, Dolores and Rose Marie (Angus) Cardona for allowing my sisters and me to have a great childhood. You spoiled us and you gave us everything we wanted along with a lot of love. Thanks for being there when sickness had me down. Thanks for the books, which allowed me to wonder, to think, and to dream beyond what was to what could be. Thanks for my childhood mom and dad.

Thanks to my sisters Lola and Linda for all the good memories I have of us growing up together. We had fun and love. We had good times and we had bad times but we always loved each other. Thanks for being there when I was sick. Thanks to their children Donnie and Daniella, Marley and Shea. Thanks to my brother, Charles (Carlos Cardona) Longsworth. We grew up apart but thanks for being my brother. Also thanks to his children: Vanica, Omar, Charles, Michael and Vanessa.

To my wife Wanda Cardona, I owe so much thanks to you. It does not matter where or how our journey takes us, some facts are irrefutable. When I was sick, and cancer (both times) had me down to skin and bones, you along with the rest of my family, gave me the love and care that saved my life. But it was you above all who nursed me back to life on a daily basis. It was you did for me all the things I could not do physically do for myself, and you did it all with unconditional love.

When I recovered (both times) and told you my life had changed forever you understood. When I said I wanted to live out all my dreams you said, "knock yourself out". ☺ When I said I did not want to work permanent jobs anymore and do only temp jobs then take off for months at a time, you said "I got the bills covered". I said I wanted to travel for months at a time and live life on my terms while volunteering with the children and you said go for it. When I wanted to make a movie, you bought me the camera. When I told you that I wanted to write this book, you bought me a computer. I thank you.

To my son Randy Cardona Jr., I thank you because you made it easy and fun to be a father and according to you I was "an excellent father". If that is all I have to show at the end of my life, it was definitely worth it. We did everything together and we played every game thousands of times and each time was exciting. I was not the perfect father but I understood how important your childhood was and that I only had one chance. We did it kid and it was you made me look good by being a great son. Thanks.

To my granddaughters Kayla, Kamyce and Katirya, thanks for being there for me. Thanks for the respect and love you give me every time we meet. You three are the best grand- daughters a person could possibly have in their life.

I thank Alton Cooper, mayor of Utila in 2010, for giving me the opportunity to work with the children in sports and education for one great year of my life. It was on this trip that I connected again with the uniqueness of growing up on Utila and decided to finish writing this story.

I have to thank MSC Industrial Supply where I was fortunate to work with the best group of individuals and organization. It was while working at MSC Industrial Supply that I got the offer from the mayor of Utila in 2010 to work with the children. Everyone wished me well and said they understood. I do not know how or when my career at MSC will end but I do know that it was a must stop in my journey through life.

Acknowledgements

In writing this book, I have to give special thanks to three people whose memories of names and events were crucial: Wanda Cardona, Tonia Woods and Mannie (Elridge) Coburn. Without their help I would have to leave out much of the book. Thanks also go to Lola (Cardona) Bernard, Harley Gregory, Paul Alan Viera, Edward McKenzie, Elden Bush, Sarita Herrera, Connie (Zuniga) Castro, Rose Smith, Marie Cardona and Grace (Hinds) James for their help.

CPSIA information can be obtained at www.ICGtesting.com
Printed in the USA
BVOW06s0623221115

428056BV00014B/488/P